# WITH THE WORD

## A BIBLE STUDY AND DEVOTIONAL GUIDE FOR GROUPS OR INDIVIDUALS

D1714377

Faith & Life
Resources

Harrisonburg, VA and Waterloo, ON

# Table of contents

# Introduction

Welcome to *With the Word*! This exciting new series from Faith & Life
Resources invites you to draw closer to God by spending time with the Word
through Bible study and daily devotions.

## Studying Luke

All the New Testament Gospels tell the story of Jesus, but each does so in
its own unique way. As in Matthew and Mark, Jesus' ministry in the Gospel
of Luke centers on the reign of God. In his words and deeds, Jesus ushers in
this reign of God, even as its final fulfillment lies in the future. Jesus begins
his ministry in Galilee, gathers disciples, heals the crowds, and teaches people what it means to follow him. He eventually travels to Jerusalem, where he
suffers, dies, and is raised from the dead.

In telling this story of Jesus, the writer of the Gospel of Luke emphasizes
certain themes more than others and includes stories and teachings not
found in the other Gospels. Luke tells the story of Jesus' birth in Bethlehem, with the angels and shepherds to witness the event. He also recounts
the parallel birth story of John the Baptist, another child divinely com-
missioned for a task. In his inaugural sermon in Nazareth, Jesus claims to
fulfill the promises of Isaiah 61; he is the Anointed One who will liberate
the oppressed. The Jesus of Luke's Gospel pays special attention to the poor,
the lowly, the outcast, and many teachings highlight issues of wealth and
poverty. Jesus calls disciples to follow him and sends them out to participate
in his mission of preaching and healing. The Jesus of Luke's Gospel eats with
diverse people, both religious leaders and sinners, demonstrating that God's
salvation is available to all. At these meals he invites his listeners to be as
generous in their hospitality as God is.

The Jesus of Luke's Gospel continues to invite people now, as he did then, to be part of God's reign and to participate in God's mission of salvation by becoming disciples.

—from Sheila Klassen-Wiebe, *Gather 'Round* Bible insight essay (Brethren Press, Elgin, IL, and MennoMedia, Harrisonburg, VA), Winter 2010. Used by permission.

# Session format

* * * * * * * * * * * * * * * * * * * * * * * * * * * * * * * * *

In this volume on Luke, you will find eight sessions for either group or individual use. The easy-to-use format starts with an in-depth Bible study and ends with seven short devotionals designed to be read in the days after the session. Here's a guide to each session:

- **Opening:** The opening of the Bible study portion calls you into the session through a summary of the text and a few questions for reflection. Before you begin each session, take time to read the text reflectively.

- **For the leader:** These are ideas for how to use the material in a group setting. If using the material individually, omit this section.

- **Understanding God's Word:** This section makes connections between the session's text and today's world.

- **Connecting with God's Word:** This is the heart of the guide; it's the in-depth Bible study that calls you to examine specific parts of the session's text. The writer gives background for a few verses of text, then outlines a series of questions for personal reflection or discussion. These questions always invite you to make connections between the biblical text and your own life.

- **Closing:** The Bible study portion of the session then closes with a brief time of worship and wrapping up.

- **Devotionals:** Immediately after the sessions you will find seven short devotionals on the session's text. Each devotional starts with a Scripture verse, includes a meditation, and ends with a prayer. Use these seven inspiring devotionals in the days after the session as way to keep the text in your heart and mind.

Spend time *With the Word* today!

# Rewards of faithfulness

LUKE 1:5-38

* * * * * * * * * * * * * * * * * * * * * * * * * * * * * * * * * * *

## Opening

The angel Gabriel appeared to Zechariah and then to Mary. Mary's visit upstages Zechariah's. Were you greeted by an angel when you felt God's presence? How did it change your life?

## Understanding God's Word

Luke stresses that salvation is rooted in the faith and longings of Israel. In Zechariah and Elizabeth (vv. 5-25), we find the best of faith and personal longings.

Verses 26-38 describe the angel's meeting with Mary, announcing that she will become pregnant and give birth to Jesus. Jesus will establish a new eternal kingdom in the lineage of David.

Catholics meditate on Mary's lack of sin. Uniquely "full of grace," she was the only fit vessel for the Son of God. For Protestants, grace is central; it is "unmerited favor." What did Luke want us to understand—Mary's questions or Mary's obedience?

## Connecting with God's Word

### Both were upright in the sight of God (1:5-7)
Both Zechariah and Elizabeth were members of priestly families. They were

* * * * * * * * * * * * * * * * * * * * * * * * * * * * * * * * * * *

## For the leader

When has God come near to you? Share your story so that class members will also share.

1. In prayer, thank God for entering the lives of class members. Sing a gathering hymn.

2. Read Luke 1:5-38. Assign readers: verses 5-7; 8-20; 21-25; 26-38. Listen closely to the conversation of the angel Gabriel with Zechariah and with Mary.

accorded the highest tribute for a faithful Israelite—"righteous before God, living blamelessly according to all of the commandments" (v. 6).

Yet God did not bless them with children. They were vulnerable, since the care of the elderly was the responsibility of the children.

- How do you see the disparity between a life of faith and not realizing goals and dreams?

- In what ways does your family care for its older members?

### Zechariah's division was on duty (1:8-10)
The twenty thousand priests and Levites around Jerusalem were divided into twenty-four divisions. Each division served in the temple twice a year, performing sacrifices, caring for the candlesticks, and burning incense.

By lot, Zechariah earned the privilege of burning incense. His was a once-in-a-lifetime opportunity.

- Describe a "once-in-a-lifetime" event that your church treasures. Or tell the story of one who made a major change in response to God's call.

- What duties do you carry in your congregation? Do you look forward to fulfilling them?

### Gabriel, an angel of the Lord, appeared to him (1:11-15a)
In the temple, Zechariah breathed to God the couple's great longing. Then Gabriel appeared to calm his fears. He affirmed that God had heard his prayer. Elizabeth would give birth to a son named John. "Many will rejoice," the angel said, "because of his birth" (v. 14).

- How has the story of Zechariah and Elizabeth helped couples who have struggled with infertility?

- Describe the joy you experienced when you knew that your prayer would be answered.

### In the sixth month, God sent the angel Gabriel to Nazareth (1:26-27)
Gabriel now appeared to Mary. She had exchanged vows with Joseph, a descendant of David, but had not yet moved to his home.

- What does the visit of Angel Gabriel to Mary, a woman, suggest about her key role in salvation history? How are the insights and gifts of women recognized in your church?

### Greetings, favored one! (1:28-33)
This passage is full of "grace" (Greek *charis*). The common greeting, "You who are highly favored," translates into one Greek word, *kecharitomene*.

Mary was "much perplexed." She would become pregnant and bear a son, to be named Jesus. He would be great, Son of the Most High, and would sit on David's throne to rule over the house of Jacob in an eternal kingdom.

- The Advent season can be a time to "listen to our longings." How do we test whether our call from God is within our longings and hopes?

### How will this be, since I am a virgin? (1:34-37)

Gabriel's answer moved the miracle of Mary's pregnancy beyond everyone's expectations. The child would be the result of the creative agency of the Holy Spirit. The terms "will come upon you" and "will overshadow you" (v. 35) do not have sexual connotations: the first appears at Pentecost (Acts 1:8), the second with the cloud at the Transfiguration (Luke 9:34).

The Spirit's action was the source of the child's significance: "Therefore the child to be born will be holy; he will be called the Son of God" (v. 35). The angel divulged the wonder being fashioned in Mary's relative Elizabeth, demonstrating that "nothing will be impossible with God" (v. 37).

- Our experiences with the divine are seldom as dramatic as Mary's, yet we know of genuine encounters with God. How do we cultivate such openness?

- Have you experienced tension between your desire to know and your sense of what God is doing?

### Here am I, servant of the Lord (1:38)

Mary's willingness to accept her role is unique: "Let it be with me according to your word." Protestant stress on God's unmerited grace may overlook this view of Mary. Heirs of the Anabaptists see Mary as the first and model disciple. When Jesus learns that his family wishes to see him, he replies, "My mother and brothers are those who hear the word of God and do it" (8:21). When the disciples await the birth of the church, "Mary, the mother of Jesus" (Acts 1:14) is among them.

- As we respond to God's word, we become like Mary, bearers of Christ to the world. Listen for God's word to you. Believe that God hears and accepts your responses.

## Closing

1. Recall the expectations at the birth of your child, your grandchild, or your friend's newborn.

2. Close by reading Luke 1:26-38. Thank God that Mary's obedience brought to us the Savior.

# DEVOTIONALS

* * * * * * * * * * * * * * * * * * * * * * * * * * * * * * * *

## Devotional 1

*[Zechariah and Elizabeth] were righteous before God, living blamelessly. . . . But they had no children. —Luke 1:6-7*

A young couple was awash in tears. Five years ago, I'd performed their wedding. Now they were grieving, broken. They discovered they would never have biological children. Their dreams of a family were shattered. Most couples are able to bear children naturally. For those who are childless, life seems unfair.

Zechariah and Elizabeth are childless in a culture where children are a sign of God's blessing. Since they are blameless and godly, shouldn't God honor their desire? But God doesn't until the angel appears in the temple.

You may also know the pain of not receiving what you deserve. Your dreams are broken, hopes shattered. The angel's visit to Zechariah affirms that God does not leave us discouraged. We may not have an angel visitor, but God cares and will meet our needs.

The couple was able to adopt and fulfill their dream of a family. God hears and acts; that's the lesson of this text. *–Jim Holm*

*I have great hopes, too, Lord. Help me trust your care, even in the dark places when hope seems gone. I know you hear; please let me feel your love, wherever the path may lead.*

* * * * * * * * * * * * * * * * * *

## Devotional 2

*[Zechariah] was chosen by lot, according to the custom of the priesthood, to enter the sanctuary of the Lord and offer incense. —Luke 1:9*

The T.V. ad features a man standing on a street corner holding his umbrella. A voice says, "You may think your chances of winning a lottery are like the odds of being struck by lightning." At that moment the man is zapped, and his umbrella is a smoking skeleton.

Zechariah is chosen by "chance" to enter the sanctuary to offer incense. This way of assigning the coveted task was like pulling names from a hat to decide who will serve.

At first it seems that Zechariah simply has "good luck." He anticipates the experience as a spiritual highlight. But this event has greater significance. While in the holy place, an angel visits Zechariah, announcing the promise of a son for him and Elizabeth.

Good things come unexpectedly. We can label them "good luck" or coincidence, but faith and reflection teach us otherwise. The way the pieces fit into place show that God is at work. In what ways do "chance" events reveal God's provision and love for you? *–Lynn Graham*

*Fill each step of my journey with anticipation, O God. Assure me that you are setting out a way for your plan to unfold.*

* * * * * * * * * * * * * * * * * *

## Devotional 3

*[John the Baptist] will . . . turn the hearts of parents to their children, and the disobedient to the wisdom of the righteous. —Luke 1:17*

When your heart turns and points, do people say, "Don't point that thing at me!" Or does your heart point others to the grace in Jesus' birth?

I must allow God to turn me toward being

as innocent as a child, rather than cynical and doubting. Though the latter may be easier—as it was for Zechariah—I believe that at Christ's birth new opportunities came for him to be born in our hearts and relationships.

It is hard to believe that the hearts of adults would turn toward a child, that erring souls would turn to wisdom. A social worker places children from neglectful homes into foster care. A therapist deals with the mentally ill. Teachers deal with rival gangs. They ask, "When will this day dawn?"

The power of love strengthens my belief that the day is still dawning. John's mandate, "to make ready a people prepared for the Lord" (v. 17), is still working its mysterious power in the hearts of people today.
—Craig Morton

*Shake from me the cynical expectations for the worst in my world to happen, and replace the doubt with hope that your Word will not return to you fruitless.*

* * * * * * * * * * * * * * *

## Devotional 4

*This is what the Lord has done for me.*
—Luke 1:25

Annie M'Bwana, 23, cuddled her tiny son in a room with women theologians, students, and church leaders from six African countries.

In 2002, Annie heard that African women theologians would meet in Bulawayo, Zimbabwe. She was determined to join them. With little money Annie managed to get a flight to Zimbabwe. Due to red tape at the Harare airport, she and wee Jacob missed their connecting flight. The next morning Barbara, a Brethren in Christ sister, put them on a train to Bulawayo.

At the conference, Annie heard African women tell of struggles to be trained

theologically and to be recognized as church leaders. Their stories encouraged her to pursue her studies and the work to which God had called her.

In Luke's story, Elizabeth endured a long journey of delays, disgrace, and despair. Like Sarah, Rachel, and Hannah before her, she begged God for a son. God heard and answered her prayer. Even in "seclusion" she proclaims the goodness of God.
—Ferne Burkhardt

*You are my God, and I will give thanks to you; you are my God, I will extol you. (Psalm 118:28)*

* * * * * * * * * * * * * * *

## Devotional 5

*You will conceive in your womb and bear a son, and you will name him Jesus.*
—Luke 1:31

I remember the moment when a drugstore box test told me that I was pregnant with my second child. It was news I wanted to receive.

Mary's story is different. She discovers she is "with child" when an unexpected messenger from God tells her the news. Her reaction, "perplexed," is an understatement. Speechless, dumbfounded, or stunned is more accurate. Yet Mary has the courage to continue the conversation. She listens to the angel and accepts this amazing news.

God may speak in more conventional modes, through a box, as it were. We hear God in the awe of worship, through powerful Scriptures, and in the magnificence of nature.

But sometimes God catches us off guard. A family member, a sales clerk, a hymn speaks to us in a new way. We are perplexed. What does this mean? What does God want me to hear? How should I respond? To whatever message, we hear the same encouragement as the angel to Mary: "Don't be afraid." —*Jayne Byler*

*Open our ears and our eyes today, Lord, to hear you speaking to us. May we listen outside the box for your more perplexing calls.*

* * * * * * * * * * * * * *

## Devotional 6

*For nothing will be impossible with God.* —*Luke 1:37*

My friend found for her fiancé a one-bedroom apartment near her house—perfect, since they would share a car. That he didn't have a job didn't seem to worry her. "If it's God's will, it will work out," she said.

He settled in and applied for an auto mechanic position. The job market was rather dismal, but by the middle of the week he had landed a job.

My friend's statement of faith echoed Mary's. For the second time, an angel of the Lord delivered an early, shocking birth announcement, this time to Mary. The angel assured her, "Nothing will be impossible with God."

While Mary was surprised, she believed that God would bring it about. God's will is much stronger than any other she could imagine. God could create miracles—even a virgin birth—to accomplish God's mission. Mary simply accepted that if it is God's will, there will be a way, for nothing is impossible with God! —*Jill Landis*

*God, if your will involves "impossibilities," grant us faith to wait for those things to happen. Let us, with Mary, believe that nothing will be impossible for you!*

* * * * * * * * * * * * * *

## Devotional 7

*Mary said, "Here am I, the servant of the Lord; let it be with me according to your word." —Luke 1:38*

At nineteen I was working in refugee camps in Thailand. I thought I was taking time off from school to figure out what I wanted to study. The work was mundane, but the experience was extraordinary.

Midway through my term, it happened for me. Standing in a building with walls of mesh wire, a roof of corrugated metal, and surrounded by bags of milk powder, I knew that I was called to church work. I assumed it meant working with refugees, but that was not the case. Living into my calling did not come for years.

In that warehouse I was not sure to what I was saying yes. But I was primed to say yes because my faith community had prepared me. They told stories of people who said yes to God in many ways. They supported those who said yes in ways large and small. It taught the liberating gospel of Jesus.

Did Mary know to what she was saying yes? Perhaps not, but something prepared her to say yes. —*Regina Shands Stoltzfus*

*God, I am grateful that you call your people to participate in your work in the world. Equip me to hear you speak and then to respond with my whole heart.*

# Hope for those who suffer

LUKE 1:39-56

## Opening

Display artwork of Mary singing the Magnificat. Invite one member to read verses 39-45 as preparatory to the Magnificat. Then listen to verses 46-55. Ask, "What captures your attention?" Share with the class.

## Understanding God's Word

Mary visits Elizabeth after Gabriel's visit to her (Luke 1:39-56). At her arrival Elizabeth greets Mary with a prophetic speech (vv. 42-45), acclaiming her as the mother of Jesus. She blesses Mary for her trust in the angel's message.

In response Mary sings the Magnificat (vv. 46-55). She praises God for being chosen for this exalted position. She affirms that God is fulfilling his promise to Israel through her. Mary predicts that the existing social order will be changed and that salvation will be available to all lowly and oppressed peoples.

## Connecting with God's Word

***Mary got ready and hurried to . . . Zechariah's home (1:39-45)***
Fired with faith in what she has heard about herself and Elizabeth (v. 36), Mary hurried to a "Judean town in the hill country" (v. 39) where Zechariah

---

### For the leader

Bring artwork of Mary singing the Magnificat.

1. Give thanks to God for making his presence known to class members this past week.

2. Sing "My Soul Proclaims the Wonder," number 181 in *Hymnal: A Worship Book* (Scottdale, Pa.: Mennonite Publishing House, 1992).

and Elizabeth lived. Entering Elizabeth's home, Mary greeted her and broke her cousin's six months of seclusion.

Elizabeth felt her baby leap within her. Earlier, Gabriel had told Zechariah that his son would "before birth be filled with the Holy Spirit" (v. 15). Elizabeth knew that Mary was pregnant, and that both mother and child were "blessed" (v. 42).

Within this ecstatic exchange, Elizabeth confessed that she was honored by the visit of "the mother of my Lord" (v. 43). Elizabeth knew what the disciples would learn after their association with Jesus. In recognition of this, verse 44 tells us Elizabeth's baby "leaped for joy." In the womb, John the Baptist carried out his mission of identifying Jesus, heralding the Messiah's reign.

- Mary's experience focused on what would fulfill divine promises, such as how Mary would nurture Jesus, and how Jesus would conduct his ministry. What vision is guiding your life? What goals are guiding the ministry of your church?

- How do you nurture children toward faith in Jesus Christ? How does the congregation assist and mentor children? What church activities benefit children?

### Mary's song (1:47-56)

Mary's song comes between the birth announcements and the deliveries of John and Jesus. The visit of the two divinely chosen women, Mary and Elizabeth, inspired soaring verse and the unborn to dance.

In Mary's song, the small and grand scales of God's work converge. Mary acknowledges that she received the promise from the angel and the resulting pregnancy as a blessing. The song praises God for the massive "upside-downing" of all things. God cared for Mary's humble status. And God is also upsetting hierarchical class systems and oppressive governments. Mary's story is a microcosm of the holy story, which includes her ancestors, Abraham and Israel.

An important feature of Mary's song is the tense of the verbs. Referring to God's activity, she uses the past tense: "He has . . ." It looks back to God's mighty deeds. But it also looks forward to the unfolding of what God has begun through Mary. Yet "so sure is the singer that God will do what is promised that it is proclaimed as accomplished fact" (Fred B. Craddock. *Luke.* Interpretation Commentary. Louisville: John Knox, 1990, 30).

Mary's song concludes (v. 55) by affirming that God's sending of Jesus is not a new promise but an old promise kept. Her son will usher in a long-awaited age that is not merely "spiritual" but in which social and political systems will be set aright. Jesus will fulfill Israel's eternal hopes.

- Many Christians don't know what to do with Mary. Some venerate her as the "Queen of Heaven." Others downplay her role. In order to avoid venerating her, have we missed her teaching about discipleship?

- How do you view Mary? How has her life affected your faith? How does your congregation give attention to Mary's life and lifestyle?

Mary was the first disciple of Jesus. She is a model for us on how to receive, act upon, and proclaim the gospel. Raymond E. Brown (*A Coming Christ in Advent*, Liturgical Press, 1988, 60-61) suggests that *first*, Mary was the first to hear the gospel, as Gabriel presented it to her. *Second*, Mary was the first to recognize her own part in the gospel story by saying, "Here I am, the servant of the Lord; let it be with me according to your word" (v. 38). And *third*, Mary was the first to proclaim the gospel through her song of praise, the Magnificat (1:46-55).

- How does your view of Mary affect the way you listen to God's voice and carry it out?

- In what ways has Mary's song influenced your congregational witness?

- Kathleen Norris says, "We cling to what we know. . . . But God keeps calling and, surprisingly . . . it is the barren Hannahs, the young Davids, and innocent Marys who hear, believe, and further God's reign. As many times as we turn away from their witness, God has put us together on the road to Jerusalem. It is never the right time, and we are never ready. . . . Once we say: 'Here am I, the servant of the Lord,' the angel will depart and the path will open before us" (*Christian Century*, Dec. 13, 2005, 18). Name a time when your congregation said, "Here we are: servants of the Lord." How did the path open up?

## Closing

1. Invite class members to share how Mary's song has encouraged them to walk in new ways of Christian discipleship.

2. Close by reading the Magnificat (vv. 46-55). Pray that the Spirit of God will inspire and provide insight on living for Christ this week.

# DEVOTIONALS

* * * * * * * * * * * * * * * * * * * * * * * * * * * * * * * * * * *

## Devotional 1

*Mary set out and went with haste to a Judean town in the hill country, where she entered the house of Zechariah and greeted Elizabeth. —Luke 1:39-40*

One of the first voices that made me believe God could use me in church work came during my Voluntary Service assignment in San Francisco. Pastor Lois encouraged me to consider seminary and congregational leadership. This was a call I tested over the years. It was the beginning that became reality.

Mary, in her newly pregnant state, hastens to Elizabeth to be somewhere safe and supportive. She wants to hear words of encouragement. She wishes to go to someone who will not judge or gossip about her.

And Elizabeth does not disappoint. She greets Mary with words of blessing and confirmation. Mary responds in a magnificent song of praise.

Without those words from Lois, what other career would I have chosen? Without the words from Elizabeth, how would Mary endure her scandalous pregnancy? Without your words of encouragement, what call from God might be missing? All of us can act as an encouraging Elizabeth to the perplexed Marys in our lives. *—Jayne Byler*

*I don't always know the right thing to say to those in need, Lord. Today give me a word of encouragement that I might speak to someone dear to me.*

## Devotional 2

*Blessed are you among women, and blessed is the fruit of your womb. —Luke 1:42*

What surprises me in Luke 1–2 is that the Holy Spirit seems to descend on almost everyone! The Spirit is on Zechariah, Elizabeth, Mary, Simeon, and Anna. It rests upon the young and the old.

Also striking is that when someone has the Holy Spirit, they start blessing people. Elizabeth blesses Mary and the fruit of her womb. Mary acknowledges God's blessing on her and through her the whole people of Israel. Zechariah blesses God and the people of Israel. Simeon and Anna offer their blessings.

Holy Spirit-filled congregations should expect many blessings. A young adult shared that she was headed to a mission program in Africa but was nervous about her decision. Later I overheard an older adult talking with her about her own experience as a young woman, second-guessing her decision to go to Brazil as a missionary. "Just go where you think God wants you, and you'll do the right thing." I felt blessed at overhearing that conversation. *—Carol Penner*

*Lord, Sunday as we gather for worship, fill us with your Holy Spirit, so that we may give and be a blessing to everyone who enters.*

* * * * * * * * * * * * * *
## Devotional 3

*Blessed is she who believed that there would be a fulfillment of what was spoken to her by the Lord. —Luke 1:45*

There's a big difference between promises made and promises kept. Politicians make promises; athletes and coaches make promises for their team's success; and advertisers promise consumers good health and great satisfaction for their products.

We make promises—to our spouse, our children, and our friends. Promises are easy to make. They roll off the tongue like butter off a hot roll. But keeping them—that's another story.

Mary receives an incredible promise—that she will be the mother of our Lord. When she meets her cousin Elizabeth, the latter recognizes the promise and blesses Mary for believing it.

You may be living in the middle of a broken promise, one made to you or one you made to another. You may be disappointed, discouraged, and full of anxiety or even grief. In the midst of these there is the promise of one whose word cannot be broken. Like Mary, we can believe that the Lord will do what he says. *–Jim Holm*

*Lord, I know the difference between promises made and promises kept. Help me to keep my promises and to rely on you to keep yours.*

* * * * * * * * * * * * * *
## Devotional 4

*My soul magnifies the Lord, and my spirit rejoices in God my savior. —Luke 1:46*

I first heard "My soul is filled with joy" when I attended the 2003 Mennonite World Conference in Zimbabwe. The tune emerged accompanied by strings, flutes, and guitar. The harmony was exquisite. The lyrics proclaimed the joy of God's promise to provide food for the hungry and to remember his chosen people.

When I returned home, it was the first song I played on my guitar. Two years later, during a seminary Advent service we turned to the same song. Then I realized that the words were a rendition of Mary's song of praise.

Mary's praise spontaneously flowed out of her. I have had those special moments when God answered a prayer or when a long awaited event occurred.

Each Christmas I anticipate singing Mary's song to let it remind me of the times the song has touched me. Mostly I will remember the way the praise flowed out of another young woman who experienced life-changing, long-awaited news. *–Jill Landis*

*"My soul is filled with joy, as I sing to God my savior. He has looked upon his servant; he has visited his people. . . . Holy is his name."*

* * * * * * * * * * * * * *
## Devotional 5

*My soul magnifies the Lord, and my spirit rejoices in God my Savior. . . He has scattered the proud in the thoughts of their hearts. —Luke 1:47, 51*

E. Stanley Jones calls Mary's Magnificat "the most revolutionary document in the world." While the words are couched in the present, it prophesies about the future. And God continues to demonstrate power. God scatters the proud . . . casts down the powerful . . . exalts the lonely . . . fills the hungry, and . . . sends the rich away empty. During the Christmas season it is reassuring for believers to hear and know the promise that evil will fail, by the God who took on human flesh that night in Bethlehem.

The Christmas season reminds us that many things are not like they seem. Jesus, despite his humble birth, becomes King of Kings. The once-powerful Herod dies a horrible death. The shepherds, derided by their fellow citizens, become ardent worshippers. God has a wonderful way of demonstrating mighty power and enduring compassion. That same God works today! *—Marvin Hein*

*Lord, reassure me that you have not ceased to upset the deception of those who oppose you and your people. Help my unbelief!*

* * * * * * * * * * * * * *

## Devotional 6

*My soul magnifies the Lord, and my spirit rejoices in God my Savior. —Luke 1:47*

In the summer of 2003, my wife and I entertained a young couple in our home. During their visit, they expressed deep disappointment at not being able to conceive children. We sympathized with them and hoped that their wish would come true. Imagine the joy on the husband's face when he stopped by later to tell me that his wife was expecting.

Luke's Gospel conveys the same sense of surprise and joy. Elizabeth, with no hope of becoming a mother, now was expecting a child. Her joy multiplied when Mary came to visit carrying a child. Both were aware that God had made their pregnancies possible. The events surrounding the conception of their children led them to believe that their offspring were destined for great things. In response, Mary magnified God in a declaration of praise.

Mary's song did not speak of her unborn son, but of God's action. God, who orchestrated the birth of their children, planned for the good fortunes of their nation. The God who rescued Elizabeth from the shame of barrenness shows mercy to all generations that fear God. *—Ervin R. Stutzman*

*Loving savior of all people, thank you for showing your goodness to us though your servants Elizabeth and Mary.*

* * * * * * * * * * * * * *

## Devotional 7

*My soul magnifies the Lord . . . for he has looked with favor on the lowliness of his servant. —Luke 1:46-48*

In Scripture, God's blessings frequently come through women of faith. Consider Jesus' birth. Those who first worshipped Christ were Mary, Elizabeth, and Anna. Mary believed the impossible and sacrificed her reputation to be used by God. Her "yes" to God (v. 38) represents the essence of Christian discipleship.

Long-suffering Elizabeth, "filled with the Holy Spirit" (v. 41), joyfully blessed the baby in Mary's womb. Her delight in the Savior and her willingness to recognize in Mary an even greater gift than her own, show humility and worship.

The widow Anna, an elderly prophet in love with the Lord, received her lifelong desire—an encounter with the Messiah (2:38). Her zeal in proclaiming the good news demonstrates what happens when we have a clear vision of Jesus.

In a culture that considered women unreliable and inferior, God proclaimed these three—and women after them—to be channels of the good news. Be enriched by their testimonies. Be open to the ways in which godly women today bless the Lord. *—Leslie Hawthorne Klingler*

*With Mary we magnify you, Lord; with Elizabeth we joyfully bless you as Savior; and with Anna we proclaim our encounter with you.*

# A wondrous birth

LUKE 2:1-20

* * * * * * * * * * * * * * * * * * * * * * * * * * * * * *

## Opening

The story of Jesus' birth is told from Mary's viewpoint. While shepherds hasten, search, find, tell, praise, and return to work, Mary treasures, stores, ponders, and sifts. During the Christmas season how do we balance the outward activities with our inner reflections about their meaning?

## Understanding God's Word

God's concern for the poor and oppressed is expressed in the birth of Jesus and in the announcement to the shepherds. Angels, God's messengers, surround Jesus' birth with songs of praise and shalom. Shepherds go, see, and tell the good news. Many are amazed and astonished. Mary ponders the meaning of these events.

## Connecting with God's Word

### Caesar Augustus and the birth of Jesus (2:1-5)

Luke invites us to see the birth in continuity with Israel's past. This story is set in its political context. The emperor Octavian, named Caesar Augustus, reigns. The census was for the purposes of taxation and conscription. The Jews were exempt from military service.

* * * * * * * * * * * * * * * * * * * * * * * * * * * * * *

## For the leader

Bring a birth announcement.

1. Praise God for the coming of a babe into our world. Thank God that the incarnation was understood by shepherds and by Mary. Recognize that we share in this miracle today. Pray for one another. Sing a gathering Christmas hymn.

2. Read Luke 2:1-20. Invite one member to read this account. Say, "Listen like you are hearing Luke's story for the first time." Ask what they heard. Compare this "birth announcement" with those shared today.

The census required all males to register in their ancestral homes. The journey from Nazareth "up" to Bethlehem (elevation 2,500 feet/762 meters) was about 80 miles/130 kilometers through the mountains of Samaria and past Jericho. Luke reveals the hand of God working through political affairs for divine purposes.

- Caesar Augustus represents the summit of Roman rule. He was the first emperor, hailed as "savior of the whole world" and called "divine son." Caesar's birthday, September 23, was celebrated as the beginning of the good news for the world. Today, how do authorities impact the way you act, think, and feel?

- Have you been required to carry out a legal mandate? How did you handle it? Did something good result for you, your family? Share your story.

### She gave birth to her firstborn son (2:6-7)
Little attention is given to the actual setting and manner of Jesus' birth. Traditions have provided an innkeeper and animals (not mentioned, but implied by the manger). Visitors to Bethlehem today are shown a cave as the site of Jesus' birth.

The "inn" (katalyma) was little more than a large room where travelers unhitched their animals in a common area in the center. Guests slept in a slightly raised platform above them. Crowded out of normal lodgings, Mary and Joseph stayed in such a shelter. Here the Messiah, the Son of the Most High, was born. In wrapping him in bands of cloth, Mary reflected the customary loving care for a newborn.

- The birth of Jesus is no private family affair. The savior is born "for all the people" and "for you" (the shepherds!). How are births recognized today? Do birth announcements appear in your church and community media? Is social media used? How do these announcements impact the parents, church, and community?

- God thinks differently from humans. In Jesus, God shows us that the Savior is not a celebrity. How would you feel about Jesus being described as a superstar? What difference does it make that Jesus is your Savior, not your celebrity?

### The shepherds and the angels (2:8-20)
Outside Bethlehem, during the night watch, an angel suddenly appeared. The shepherds were afraid—a normal reaction to an angel's appearance in biblical stories. The angel calmed their fears and announced good news. The swaddling clothes and manger were "signs" so shepherds could distinguish this newborn from others in Bethlehem.

The multitude of angels was a fraction of the "heavenly host." Their song encompassed "the highest heaven"—not just a great degree of glory—and earth, upon which it declares peace. In Hebrew, shalom (peace) was bestowed upon those on whom God's gracious favor rests. The announcement of good news came not to the imperial court but to shepherds outside a small town. With the angels' departure, the shepherds quickly obeyed their instructions.

In Bethlehem, the shepherds found Mary, Joseph, and the baby. They became evangelists for the Messiah, spreading the news to many. But Mary quietly treasured the events in her heart, pondering and sifting their significance. She learned the angels' song from the shepherds. She had already sung, "He has brought down the powerful from their thrones and lifted up the lowly" (1:52). Mary knew that great reversals would be done through her tiny baby.

"On earth peace" was not pax Romana but pax Christi, the peace that passes all understanding (Philippians 4:7). Mary's heart wouldn't give up trying to understand it.

- The shepherds returned to their jobs praising God. Do you go to work praising God? Does your workplace need more joy?

- Christmas is a time for celebration, meaning, and joy. How do you experience these moments? How does congregational worship help you center the joyous Christmas experience?

- In Matthew and Luke the poor and humble are exalted; the powerful and proud humbled. Our celebrations tend to the opposite. How can your church commemorate "on earth peace" in ways that integrate peace, rather than promote inequity and division?

- God shows us a connection between a poor baby and poor shepherds. God will save the world not from the top down but from the bottom up. That's the good news. How do you walk faithfully under God's plan? How does it encourage and empower you?

## Closing

1. Share one way the birth of Jesus has changed your life.

2. Close by reading Luke 2:16-20. Pray that each member will find a way to praise God for the birth of Jesus until the class meets again.

*Luke 2:1-20*

# Devotionals

## Devotional 1

*A decree went out from Emperor Augustus that all the world should be registered. . . . All went to their own towns to be registered.*
—Luke 2:1, 3

The Roman census could not have come at a worse time. Mary, in the last phase of her pregnancy, faced an 80 mile/130 kilometer journey from Nazareth to Bethlehem.

Joseph's inability to secure proper housing, Herod's decree to kill all babies under two, and the difficult journey to Egypt provided the setting for Jesus' birth. Yet it was the most blessed event in history.

Troubles often provide the seedbed for great blessings. A forest fire burns the low-lying brush and enables new trees to grow. Ashes from the Mount St. Helens volcano ruined paint on cars and houses, but fertilized growing crops.

Are you facing a difficult situation? Is there a taxing journey ahead of you? When troubles flood your life, remember Joseph and Mary. The greatest miracle in history was couched in the midst of trouble.
*—Marvin Hein*

*Lord, give me the confidence to believe that you work good out of difficulties and that you will perform that good work in me.*

## Devotional 2

*She gave birth to her firstborn son and wrapped him in bands of cloth, and laid him in a manger, because there was no place for them in the inn. —Luke 2:7*

Each year obligations bombard me. My boss demands attendance at company parties. On Christmas Day my family expects the latest tasty dessert. My relatives love my handmade gifts. And I always sing in the choir, help with decorations, and attend the children's program.

The inn was full when Mary and Joseph arrived in Bethlehem. How did the inn-keeper's wife deal with the public? No one was aware of the marvelous miracle taking place among the animals. Guests only knew the government required them to come to Bethlehem. They were hungry, tired, and needed attention. Surely she felt as stressed as I do about responding to extra demands.

A healing thought provided my answer: God is here while I am doing my work. Despite the overcrowded inn, God found another place for the miracle down below with the animals.

I will keep my obligation to my "guests," but I will also retreat to a quiet place where I can worship the Lord. *—Nancy Becker*

*When the demands of holiday celebrations overwhelm me, help me run to the manger and worship the child who gives me a center and a reason to rejoice.*

## Devotional 3

*The glory of the Lord shone . . . and they were terrified. —Luke 2:9b*

A terrified Jewish girl gave birth Christmas Eve in a freshly dug grave in Poland during the Nazi occupation. "Who else but the Messiah could be born in a tomb?" asked Elie Wiesel.

Fears surrounded Jesus' birth. Frightened men coughed up family member names so Caesar would not come after them with vengeance. Joseph and Mary stumbled toward a dark cave, fearing for the safe arrival of their promised child.

Shepherds endured darkness being torn open as other-worldly light blazed upon them. Then, an unknown voice said, "No fear."

When the shepherds appeared before Mary to "see this thing that has taken place" (v. 15), did they find her singing softly to the newborn child?

Perhaps she sang, "Glory, glory, glory, O Lord above all fears, all names, and stories. I'll serve you now, and ever. I'll love you, God my Savior. . ."

Perhaps the shepherds, on their return, said, "We can take this song into the darkness, for times when the stars are silent." –Doug Schulz

*Glory, glory, glory, O Lord above all fears, all names, and stories. I'll serve you now, and ever. I'll love you, God my Savior. Glory, glory . . .*

\* \* \* \* \* \* \* \* \* \* \* \* \* \*

## Devotional 4

*Do not be afraid; for see—I am bringing you good news of great joy for all the people. —Luke 2:10*

Imagine Jesus' birth today. A birth in a germ-laden animal shelter is unthinkable. A visit to the birthing room by strangers is against the rules.

When we became grandparents, we needed to learn new rules. We felt like brand-new parents. We were required to buy an infant car seat, which arrived with an instructional video. We needed to visit our local fire station for an inspection to make sure our precious grandchild was safely strapped in place.

Today we must guard against many scary possibilities. Children cannot be left alone. We teach children not to speak to strangers. We have our children fingerprinted and arrange for a photo ID.

Though the ancient birth story seems quaint, the angels' message still applies: Don't be afraid. God has broken through our barriers of paranoia with a Savior who provides a better way to live. Calm and peace amid the fear—these are good tidings indeed. –Nancy Becker

*Today I pray for peace in the midst of terror. May all of us—children and adults—experience love and caring, not fear.*

\* \* \* \* \* \* \* \* \* \* \* \* \* \*

## Devotional 5

*There was with the angel a multitude of the heavenly host, praising God. —Luke 2:13*

Pictures of "living on a planet afloat in space," as Richard Lewis puts it, came from space missions in the 1960s. We watched humans travel to the moon and, through their cameras, look back at earth from viewpoints never seen before.

The earth "in one whole shot is amazing," said Apollo 12's Al Bean. "What a privilege," exclaimed Jim Irwin of Apollo 15, "to see the earth in its entirety."

The shepherds' encounter with the angels reflects an amazing shift in understanding. It changes the way they see both heaven and earth. They know there are stars; now angels, too. They know their fields and flocks, now they see the long-awaited Messiah. They respond with astonishment, fear, and great joy.

Can we see this new reality in the Bethlehem birth? Can we enter into the transformed view that Jesus' birth ignited? Can we sing along with the angels' excitement as they share the news? –*Dora Dueck*

*"Glory to God in the highest heaven, and on earth peace among those whom he favors!" (v. 14)*

## Devotional 6

*Mary treasured all these words and pondered them in her heart. —Luke 2:19*

Who invented the Christmas rush? Was it retailers? Was it church leaders? Or was it the shepherds? After the angel's announcement, they hurry to Bethlehem to see the wonder of the Savior's birth.

It seems that only Mary has the time to "ponder" these events. She ponders the miracle of Jesus' birth, for this child is hers, yet not hers. His birth occurs in lowly circumstances, yet is announced by an angel choir. Her child is a normal baby, yet the shepherds speak of him as Messiah, the Savior.

For Mary, each step into the future is a new revelation. Mary ponders the actions of her 12-year-old son teaching in the temple (2:51). Later Mary encounters the great mystery that her child is indeed the Son of the living God.

In the rush of this day let us take time to ponder the mystery of Christ's birth. –*Michael Dick*

*Lord, help me, like Mary, to take time often to reflect on the significance of your birth. In the rush of this season, help me to treasure the mystery.*

## Devotional 7

*The shepherds returned, glorifying and praising God for all they had heard and seen, as it had been told them. —Luke 2:20*

At moments we've felt like the "good guy." At other times, we have felt and acted like the "bad guy." Then someone encourages us, and we are changed for the good.

Take the shepherds. We're accustomed to viewing them as good guys. We tout the shepherds of Luke 2 as being faithful and diligent—the first human bearers of the good news.

But in Luke's day shepherds were described as dishonest and thieving. They weren't allowed to give witness in court because they were considered deceitful. Yet to this group of ruffians the angels came, foreshadowing Jesus' dealings with prostitutes and tax collectors. The angels arrived, honoring the dishonorable, valuing those to whom society gave little value.

Luke says that the shepherds returned, reporting everything "as it had been told them"—that is, honestly. Bingo. Lives are changed. –*Helen Tellez*

*Thank you, God, for honor and blessings I don't deserve. Today, give me an opportunity to return the favor to another of your beloved children.*

# Hearing and telling good news

LUKE 2:21-52

* * * * * * * * * * * * * * * * * * * * * * * * * * * * * *

## Opening

Luke 2:21-52 describes events in the temple. The Israelites were nurtured through the observance of rituals, special days, and formed in their faith there. Read Luke 2:21-40. How does your church encourage spiritual growth and maturity in Christ? What have you observed recently?

## Understanding God's Word

Luke 2:21-40 describes Jesus at eight days. Mary and Joseph observe the rituals of sacrifice and prayer in the temple. Hopes, dreams, and fears are recognized as the faith community blesses and encourages new parents. They meet Simeon who sees baby Jesus as the promised Messiah. Simeon's song draws on the words of Isaiah. The Messiah is now for all people. We also hear a cautionary word for Mary from Anna.

Luke 2:41-52 describes Jesus at age 12. We are between Luke's "infancy narrative" and the start of Jesus' public ministry.

* * * * * * * * * * * * * * * * * * * * * * * * * * * * * *

## For the leader

Interview two young people (one boy and one girl) that show promise in spiritual understandings. Ask how they are formed in their faith, and what it means for them to live their faith every day. Share with the class.

1. Pray for eyes to see the potential of the young in your church. Pray that they will be open to the way of Christ. Remember the concerns of class members.

2. The story in Luke 2:41-52 is only recorded in Luke. How does Jesus relate to the temple leaders? What themes relate to his life mission? Name youth that exhibit spiritual understandings.

## Connecting with God's Word

### Doing things properly (2:21-24)

Mary followed the expectations of the Mosaic Law for purification (Leviticus 12:1-8) after giving birth. Since she and Joseph could not afford a lamb, they brought two small birds as their sacrifice. Mary and Joseph consecrated Jesus to God, as expected with a firstborn son.

- How do couples introduce their pregnancy and their newborn to your congregation? What is your congregational practice?

### The Holy Spirit takes center stage (2:25-28)

The Spirit moved Simeon to respond to the infant Jesus three times: The Spirit (1) rested on Simeon (v. 25); (2) revealed to Simeon that he would see "the Lord's Christ/Messiah" before he died (v. 26); and (3) moved Simeon to enter the temple courts (v. 27). In Luke's second volume, Acts, the Spirit moves the action forward.

- Describe a time when you or your congregation were guided by the Spirit.

### Simeon's Song or the Nunc Dimittis (2:29-32)

Simeon was "looking forward to the consolation of Israel" (v. 25).When he held the child he was saying: "Here he is at last. Here is God's salvation," echoing Isaiah 40:1 and 66:13.

This poem follows the servant poetry of Isaiah 42-49: Israel is God's servant with a purpose beyond itself. Isaiah refers to the coming Messiah. David L. Bartlett observes, "Precisely by being God's gift to Israel, [Jesus] is God's gift to the whole world, since Israel serves as a light that is not limited to Israel alone" (*New Proclamation*, Year B, 1999-2000, Minneapolis: Fortress Press, 1999, 51).

- How can you allow the reality and scope of God's salvation to console you and give you new energy?

- How do you implement the conviction that God's salvation is for all people?

### A troubling message (2:33-35)

Luke introduces Jesus' suffering in the infancy narrative. While Simeon blessed Mary and Joseph, it is hardly a word to describe his message to Mary! Simeon sees rejection and catastrophe, as well as salvation, in Jesus.

And a chilling word to Mary: "A sword will pierce your own soul too" (v. 35). Perhaps Mary's soul was pierced when Jesus died on the cross. Perhaps the "sword of decision" passed through Mary's soul as she made the decision to be his disciple (Raymond E. Brown, *An Adult Christ at Christmas*, Collegeville, MN: The Liturgical Press, 1978, 34-36).

- Why suffering and swords? Kathleen Norris says that "if the Scriptures don't sometimes pierce us like a sword, we're not paying close enough attention" (*The Cloister Walk*, New York: Riverhead Books, 1996, 115).

- Elderly people produce fruit (Psalm 92:14). Grandma Moses was still painting at one hundred. Arthur Rubinstein gave a great concert at Carnegie Hall at 89. At 80, Caleb was among those sent to spy out the Promised Land. And Moses led the people of Israel until his 120th year.

### Observing the rituals (Luke 2:36-38)
Anna lived at the temple. She met young couples like Mary and Joseph, coming for the first time with their baby, bewildered by the many expectations of their faith. Anna was a mentor, a good model of service and blessing to others.

- Does your congregation have a mentoring program where adults are matched with children and youth? Mentors provide a safe setting to ask questions and to consider a variety of thoughtful responses.

### The temple . . . Jesus' piety . . . Jesus' wisdom (Luke 2:40-52)
Jesus' "hidden life" before the temple incident was that he "grew and became strong; filled with wisdom; and the favor of God was upon him" (v. 40). His "hidden life" after the incident was that he returned home with his parents and lived under their authority.

Jesus continued to increase "in wisdom and in years, and in divine and human favor" (v. 52). The growing recognition of his identity and vocation did not mean he was finished maturing.

This scene (vv. 46-47) echoes in the bar mitzvah ceremony every Jewish boy observes at his thirteenth birthday. By this age, Jesus would have studied with the rabbis. He knew the Jewish scriptures and their interpretations.

- What dreams, hopes, and fears do you have for your children? Can you imagine their place in the family of faith? How will you nurture them?

- What profound insights have you seen or heard from your children?

## Closing

1. Name one promising young boy and girl who exhibit growing faith. Thank God for each one.

2. Close by reading carefully and prayerfully Luke 2:41-52.

# DEVOTIONALS

* * * * * * * * * * * * * * * * * * * * * * * * * * * *

## Devotional 1

*[Joseph and Mary] brought him up to*
*Jerusalem to present him to the Lord.*
*—Luke 2:22*

When I was a baby, my parents wanted to
dedicate me in church. Some churches considered child dedication too much like child
baptism. My parents requested dedication
since Jesus' parents dedicated him in the
temple.

Jesus was dedicated following the custom of Exodus 13:11-16 and Leviticus 12:8.
This action set the stage for the prophecies
of Simeon and Anna about Jesus.

Child dedication is important. Parents
express thanksgiving and hopes for their
child. The congregation commits to raising
the child in the love of God. We gather with
parents, lay hands on the child, and pray that
the child will love and serve God. We pray
that congregational members will model a
life that children can imitate. *—Patty Friesen*

*Teach us to keep our homes so fair, that were*
*our Lord a child once more, he might be glad*
*to share our hearth, and find a welcome at*
*our door. —Albert F. Bayly*

* * * * * * * * * * * * * * * * *

## Devotional 2

*It had been revealed to [Simeon] by the Holy*
*Spirit that he would not see death before he*
*had seen the Lord's Messiah. —Luke 2:26*

I have dated and claimed many Bible promises. When I read these verses later I sometimes say, "God, you gave me that promise
years ago, but nothing has happened."

It was many years since God had promised Simeon he would "not see death before
he had seen the Lord's Messiah." Each day
brought fulfillment closer. One day Simeon
met Mary, Joseph, and baby Jesus in the
temple. Immediately Simeon knew this baby
was the promised One.

Simeon held the child and praised God.
Then, guided by the Holy Spirit, he announced that Jesus would bring salvation to
all nations, including the Jews (vv. 31-32).

Are you waiting for an answer to
prayer? Waiting is an essential part of walking by faith. Charles Stanley said that "trust-
ing means looking beyond what we can see
to what God sees." *—Helen Grace Lescheid*

*God, give me patience to wait, for you have*
*said, "I am the Lord; in its time I will accom-*
*plish it quickly." (Isaiah 60:22)*

* * * * * * * * * * * * * * * * *

## Devotional 3

*My eyes have seen your salvation, which you*
*have prepared in the presence of all peoples.*
*—Luke 2:30-31*

Simeon's sentiments express the universal
vision of faithful souls who lift the world to
God in prayer. "On the way to God," wrote
Henri Nouwen, "we become aware of our
neighbor's needs and begin to heal each
other's wounds."

What wounds does the world bear? Consider acts of terror, atrocities, disasters, and
accidents. Every citizen needs undiminished
prayer. Those in distress require prayer
joined by acts of grace. These will help
people believe in the God of salvation.

When revelations of deplorable conditions and destructive situations exist in my world, I pray too little. And though moved to compassion about global concerns, do I make real sacrifices of time or money to challenge inequities? Do I give—as a friend put it—"not until it hurts, but until it really helps"?

We need voices of spiritual friends like Simeon and Nouwen to hold us true to our salvation. —*Doug Schulz*

*Today, I reflect on the past, Lord, and prepare for the future. Thank you for friends who echo your heartbeat for the wounded. Help me to do that too.*

\* \* \* \* \* \* \* \* \* \* \* \* \* \*

## Devotional 4

*This child is destined for the falling and the rising of many in Israel. . . . and a sword will pierce your own soul too. —Luke 2:34-35*

A plane with three teenagers and a pilot crashed in the high mountains. The group had planned to celebrate a special birthday. Parents, with high hopes for their sons, felt a sword pierce their hearts.

Parents carry dreams for their offspring, but know they live in a dangerous world. Mary and Joseph found their hopes chilled by these words of Simeon. Being Savior and being killed didn't fit! While we don't know Mary and Joseph's response, they continued their faithful care of Jesus.

We often think of blessings in the midst of trouble and fear. In this verse dreams are dampened by pain. The Lord allows us to be pruned, and that sometimes hurts.

At Christmas we sing carols and revel in gift-giving. But some know the sword-piercing side of the season. It's like hearing Simeon again with his dire prophecy. But take heart! God feels our pain. As with

Jesus' parents, God will sustain you in your bleakest moments. —*Marvin Hein*

*Lord, when we cannot understand your sometimes strange and painful ways, keep our eyes fixed on you and your unending love.*

\* \* \* \* \* \* \* \* \* \* \* \* \* \*

## Devotional 5

*There was also a prophet Anna. . . . She was of great age. . . . She never left the temple. . . . She began to praise God. —Luke 2:36-38*

Anna, a widow, was old and tired and lonely. While the bloom and strength of Anna's body had diminished, she never ceased to worship and pray. What a lovely senior woman!

A 78-year-old friend shared a wonderful experience. While walking home she saw an older woman carting some groceries and singing as if she were the only person around. When my friend stopped to talk with her, the woman said she sang because she was a Christian. My friend said she was also a believer and loved to sing. So in the sight and hearing of neighbors and passersby, they sang a hymn together.

Aging can embitter us and cause us to withdraw, but Anna didn't allow that to happen. If you are younger, stop and provide a cheerful moment to a senior in your community. You may be surprised. The senior friend might bring you cheer.

If you are older, ask yourself whether you resonate with Anna who praises God and prays in the company of God's people. If you fall short, ask God to give you a spirit of rejoicing. —*Doug Snyder*

*Oh God, we thank you for the many around us who, in their sunset years, continue to inspire and encourage us. Help us to become more like them.*

## Devotional 6

*His mother said to him, "Child, why have you treated us like this? Look, your father and I have been searching for you in great anxiety." —Luke 2:48*

Jesus is in the temple. The people who meet him are amazed, but his parents have mixed feelings. Their son is getting much attention. He seems to have forgotten their worries about him.

This story reflects the human and the divine character of Jesus. Jesus is a preteen, not realizing that his parents might be concerned about him. At the same time, Jesus' true lineage comes through with his amazing knowledge of the Scriptures.

Like many today, Jesus' parents don't "get it." They don't always understand the way teens are processing and approaching life—maybe because it's different than the way they did. Or parents forget how it was when they were young.

The good news is that Jesus made up with his parents. His mother "treasured all these things in her heart" (v. 51). Today, she would make a scrapbook.

Parents and teens, know that Jesus walks with you. The Jesus with the heartsick parents knows your heart. The Jesus who lost track of time in the temple will not lose track of you. This Jesus is in God's heavenly house, interceding for you. *–Carol Duerksen*

*Jesus, whether we are young or old, you understand us completely. Help us in our family relationships as we go about your business today.*

## Devotional 7

*Jesus increased in wisdom and in years, and in divine and human favor. —Luke 2:52*

Walking along the path, our granddaughter Maya, aged three, suddenly withdrew her hands from ours and said, "Actually I can walk by myself." And of course she could, and she did.

It's a familiar feeling. We watch our children grow up with a mixture of pride and pain. I observed this in the face of a friend at his daughter's wedding. I heard his voice crack as he blessed the couple. Children learn to walk, we learn to let go. Our children teach us, and it's never without a touch of pain.

While the world wants to keep Jesus in the manger, the Gospels don't. Finding Jesus missing after Passover, his parents—with "great anxiety"—rush back to Jerusalem to find him discussing Scripture with the rabbis. "Child," says Mary, "why have you treated us like this? Look, your father and I have been searching for you" (v. 48).

Jesus is neither disrespectful nor apologetic. "My father's business" (v. 49 KJV), Joseph realizes, doesn't involve carpentry. The episode ends with a report that Jesus, wise beyond his age, "increased in wisdom and in years."

Shouldn't I increase in more than just years? Each letting go, while painful, should deepen, increase, and make me better able to love and to release. *–Leonard Beechy*

*As today extends my life, may it also increase my wisdom. Lord, may I learn from both love and from pain that I must be about your business.*

# What is my calling?

LUKE 4:14-37

* * * * * * * * * * * * * * * * * * * * * * * * * * * * * * * *

## Opening

Luke 14:14-30 describes the reception to Jesus teaching in Nazareth. The people are angry and disappointed. In contrast, verses 31-44 describe the gracious response to Jesus' ministry in Capernaum. How does your congregation offer the good news to those on the margins?

## Understanding God's Word

Jesus preaching in Nazareth is found in Luke 4:14-30, Matthew 13:53-58, and Mark 6:1-6a. (Only Luke includes Isaiah 61:1-2 and 58:6.) All describe the people's amazement for the words from the son of a carpenter. All describe that when the people took offense, Jesus replied that a prophet was without honor in his hometown (John 6:42a also includes this response). All agree that this skeptical attitude limited Jesus' ministry.

Only Luke includes Jesus' reminder that Elijah and Elisha healed Gentiles, and recounts the angry intent to throw Jesus off the hill. Luke believes they reject Jesus because he reminds them that God's love and mercy is for all peoples, not the Jews only.

* * * * * * * * * * * * * * * * * * * * * * * * * * * * * * * *

### For the leader

Jesus' declaration is sometimes called his "Mission Statement." Provide a copy of your congregation or denomination's mission statement.

1. Give thanks that your congregation responds to God's call. Sing a gathering hymn.

2. Read Luke 14:14-37. Assign as follows: Narrator 1, vv. 14-17; Jesus, vv. 18-19; Narrator 2, vv. 20-21a; Jesus, v. 21b; Narrator 1, vv. 22-23a; Jesus, vv. 23b-27; Narrator 2, vv. 28-30; and Narrator 1, vv. 31-37.

## Connecting with God's Word

### A pivotal scene (4:16-22)

Jesus' homily at Nazareth has been called his inaugural address, mission statement, job description, or platform (John Howard Yoder, *The Politics of Jesus*, Grand Rapids, MI: Eerdmans, 1972, 34-35). Fred B. Craddock says it describes "in miniature the nature of Jesus' ministry and his rejection by his own people in contrast to his acceptance by outsiders" (*Harper's Bible Commentary*, HarperSanFrancisco, 1988, 1,020).

- Jesus claims Isaiah's vision as his own and builds on it.

- In *Healing the Purpose of Your Life* (Dennis, Matthew, and Sheila Fabricant Linn, Paulist Press, 1999), the authors believe each person has "sealed orders" from God. These orders are not actions to be done or a designated vocation. They point to a "way of being" that energizes all we do. Sheila describes her way of being as "to care for the goodness of creation"; Dennis describes his as "being a brother"; and Matt describes his as "to make things whole." What are God's "sealed orders" for you?

- Look at your congregation or denomination's mission statement. How has this mission statement shaped your congregation? How has the statement shaped your ministry?

### The text within the text (Isaiah 61:1-2a; 42:7, 58:6)

In Luke, the texts of Isaiah 61:1-2a include phrases from Isaiah 42:7 ("recovery of sight to the blind") and 58:6 ("to let the oppressed go free"). Isaiah assures readers that all will be well. The people have received the "impossible" word that it's safe to come home. Their return is a foretaste of Jubilee ("the year of the Lord's favor") when differences of rich and poor disappear and a new era of God's salvation arrives.

- Consider one from your area who has been successful elsewhere as a church leader, athlete, business entrepreneur, actor, politician, or other achiever. What response does he or she receive when returning home?

- How has this text from Isaiah/Jesus influenced your mission statement?

- Jubilee is a time of restoration and redistribution of wealth to occur every 50 years (Leviticus 25:8-55, especially 8-12). During that year (1) the land rests, (2) all debts are canceled, (3) slaves are freed, and (4) land is restored to its original owners. While it may not have been observed fully, Leviticus 25 and Isaiah 61 kept this vision alive. The sharing by the Jerusalem church in Acts is evidence that early Christians honored the economic aspects of Jubilee in urban settings. How is it practiced in your congregation?

### The response turned nasty (4:22-30)

The synagogue-goers were amazed! But things turned nasty when Jesus clarified his mission. The people wanted him to stick with the Jews only. Jesus insisted that his mandate included Gentiles. He told two stories of prophets that ministered to outsiders—Elijah's word (1 Kings 17:8-24) kept a Phoenician widow and her son alive. Elisha's word (2 Kings 5:1-19) healed a Syrian commander of leprosy. But Jesus was driven out of town.

- When a youth or a guest challenges your way of thinking or doing, are the suggestions adopted, considered, or rejected?

### Ministering with authority (4:31-37)

Jesus' words became true when the unclean demon left a man. Jesus addressed the spirit, subdued it, and got rid of it. The man was the first captive freed from oppression as promised by Jesus (v. 8).

What Jesus taught related to what he did. This was confirmed by the instant gossip that he "began to reach every place in the region" (v. 37) and "with authority and power he commands the unclean spirits, and out they come!" (v. 36).

- Words without deeds compromise authority. What is the "word on the street" about your ministries? Do your deeds undermine what you say? Do your words affirm what you do?

## Closing

1. Read Luke 4:14-37 as suggested in the Opening.

2. Pray Matthew 28:19-20 as a mission statement and a word of blessing for your church and the class:

   "We, the people of God, are called to go and make disciples of all nations, baptizing them in the name of the Father and of the Son and of the Holy Spirit, and teaching them to obey everything Jesus has commanded us. Surely God is with us always, even to the very end of the age. Amen."

* * * * * * * * * * * * * * * * * * * * * * * * * * * *

## Devotional 1

*[Jesus] stood up to read . . . : "The Spirit of the Lord is on me, because he has anointed me." —Luke 4:16-18*

After being tested, Jesus could have spoken of his personal trials at his synagogue, but he chose Isaiah's words of inspiration.

During a family reunion at Yosemite National Park we decided to take a short hike up to a scenic lookout. Since I had only sandals, I wasn't prepared for hiking. But I decided to go anyway.

Halfway up, I realized I was not seeing any beauty. I was too busy watching my feet, making sure I didn't slip or break a sandal strap. The only time I looked up was when we met people coming down. Those meetings kept me going. They encouraged us, saying, "Keep going. You are almost there. It's a gorgeous view."

As Jesus read the words of the prophet who had gone before him, we need to do the same. Today we can look up from watching our feet and hear from those who have been to the top. *–Janet Berg*

*God, I thank you for Jesus, the supreme Encourager, who meets me on the path today.*

* * * * * * * * * * * * * * * * *

## Devotional 2

*The Spirit of the Lord is upon me, because he has anointed me to bring good news to the poor. —Luke 4:18*

As we left church, the ushers handed us brown paper bags. Each had a printed grocery list. All who had jobs were encouraged to take the list when they went to buy their own groceries and fill it for a family who had lost a job. This was a ministry for members of Mennonite churches in nearby Philadelphia.

Churches have sprung up all over Philadelphia with people from all nations of the world. The Indonesian church is reaching out to newcomers among Spanish speakers. We are invited to join Christ's embrace to those who are the last ones hired and the first laid off.

These grocery bags are our means to share Jesus' good news with the poor. It is my invitation to join Jesus in God's work this week. It's part of the good news I can share! *–Sandra Drescher-Lehman*

*May this Scripture be fulfilled in my life today. Show me ways to bring good news to those who are hurting—economically, spiritually, or emotionally.*

* * * * * * * * * * * * * * * *

## Devotional 3

*All spoke well of him and were amazed at the gracious words that came from his mouth. They said, "Is this not Joseph's son?" —Luke 4:22*

Nazareth looked the same, but Jesus was different. He was filled with God's Spirit, a teacher ready for ministry.

At the synagogue Jesus read from the prophet Isaiah. Worshippers were astonished by his teaching. They whispered, "Isn't this Jesus, the son of Joseph? How can a carpenter speak so eloquently?"

Jesus did not win friends and influence people as he insisted that he could not perform miracles in Nazareth because of their skepticism. They were furious.

During his ministry Jesus experienced popularity and acceptance along with hostility and violence. Sometimes such responses occurred on the same day, in the same village, and at the same synagogue.

Speaking God's truth today may bring mixed results. For some the good news offers hope and wholeness. For others God's expectation of obedience and holy living is unwelcome and unacceptable.

God's messengers today experience both reactions. As with Jesus, we speak God's truths graciously and consistently without concern for the ever-changing public opinion. —*Nancy Witmer*

*Lord, today I want to speak your words graciously and fearlessly. May I not be swayed by public opinion but stand firmly in your truth.*

* * * * * * * * * * * * * *

## Devotional 4

*There were many widows in Israel in the time of Elijah. . . . yet Elijah was sent to none of them except to a widow at Zarephath in Sidon. —Luke 4:25-26*

The title of Thomas Wolfe's novel, *You Can't Go Home Again*, articulates a deep truth. If you have changed while away from home, then "home" is never the same.

In his hometown synagogue in Nazareth, Jesus associates himself with Elijah and Elisha (vv. 25-27). He places himself squarely within Israel's prophetic tradition. He stresses that Elijah and Elisha performed their healing miracles on non-Jews: the widow in Sidon (v. 26), present-day Lebanon, and a Syrian general, an enemy of Israel (v. 27). Jesus makes it clear: God loves Gentiles as much as Jews.

Thus Jesus will not restrict his healing touch to deserving Jews. He will extend it

to sinners, to people on the margins, and to Gentiles. By citing Isaiah, Elijah, and Elisha, Jesus reminds worshippers that a prophet reaches out to the poor, the blind, the prisoners, and the dispossessed.

Let us remember that many fellow believers suffer from oppression or poverty today. Let us also remember to extend a prophetic, healing witness to those outside the church. —*Kathleen Kern*

*Lord, keep my mind and my heart open so that I may be receptive to prophets among us who enlarge our vision of your grace and healing love.*

* * * * * * * * * * * * * *

## Devotional 5

*There were many widows in Israel in the time of Elijah. . . . yet Elijah was sent to none of them except to a widow at Zarephath in Sidon. —Luke 4:25-26*

Jesus' lesson ended abruptly. Sensing their unbelief, Jesus spoke the truth, exposing their limited vision of God's work. He reminded them of Elijah's day, when God blessed Gentiles like Naaman the Syrian and the widow of Zarephath.

The declaration that God loves outsiders and enemies turned the synagogue worshippers into a murderous mob. In one service their response moved from admiration to unbelief to rage.

The story of biblical and church history is that God calls and uses unlikely folk. It's also a theme of great Christian literature. In J. R. R. Tolkien's *The Lord of the Rings*, the small, overlooked, and simple hobbits are chosen to fulfill a great purpose: the destruction of the ring of evil.

This truth can encourage us when we feel small and insignificant. God casts the circle of divine mercy widely. If anyone re-

ceives special treatment in the kingdom, it is the humble whose hearts are right in God's sight. Can we taste and see the wideness of God's love? Can we rejoice when enemies and outsiders experience God's favor?
—Wally Sawatsky

*Search me, O God, and know my heart. . . . see if there is any wicked way in me, and lead me in the way everlasting.*
*(Psalm 139:23-24)*

* * * * * * * * * * * * * * *

## Devotional 6

*When they heard this, all in the synagogue were filled with rage. —Luke 4:28*

It was some sermon. Why was everyone so angry at what Jesus said?

Frustrated expectations infuriate people. At first everything was fine. Jesus read from Isaiah 61 and announced the fulfillment of the prophecy about good news for the poor and freedom for the captives. Everyone was "amazed at the gracious words" (v. 22).

But then Jesus turned the tables! Instead of assuming that God's promises were for Israel alone, Jesus reminded them that God's mercy belongs to all, even foreigners. And that the hometown congregation would more likely reject a prophet than claim the blessing of a prophetic word (v. 24).

The people were angry. In a few powerful words Jesus blew away their expectations. They were exposed as pious hypocrites, smugly relying on their nationality to guarantee their relationship with God.

While their violent rage is deplorable they did hear Jesus' message: God's promises extend beyond my smugness, challenging my narrow world view. If Jesus doesn't disturb my complacency, have I heard him?
—Mary Raber

*Lord Jesus, give me grace to truly hear and believe you, the one whom the prophets foretold.*

* * * * * * * * * * * * * * *

## Devotional 7

*When they heard this, [what Jesus said], all in the synagogue were filled with rage. . . . and drove him out of the town.*
*—Luke 4:28, 29*

What a turnaround for the people of Nazareth! At first they "spoke well" of Jesus; now they were in a murderous rage. Anticipating that they wanted him to repeat some miracles, Jesus replied, "You will say to me, Doctor, cure yourself! Do here what you did in Capernaum" (v. 23 paraphrased).

Jesus then threw fuel on the fire by citing examples of Gentiles who were shown God's favor—the widow at Zarephath, and Naaman the Syrian.

Immediately Jesus is shown the door and driven to a cliff where the people will silence this blasphemer. How could the people of Nazareth reject one of their own?

Pete and I were members of the same church for years. We worked closely on several projects. While I valued his commitment and insight, there were times when I wanted to show him the door.

Why is it hardest to hear the truth from those with whom we are close and know well? What does God want to say to us through them? —Keith Harder

*God, grant me the grace to accept your word even when it comes from those whom I know well.*

# Stretching our love

LUKE 10:1-42

* * * * * * * * * * * * * * * * * * * * * * * * * * * * * * * * *

## Opening

Luke 10 describes Jesus' ministry of proclamation and healing (vv. 1-24). The Good Samaritan story demonstrates that faith must respond to human need (vv. 25-37). With Mary and Martha daily life tasks are seen within one's relationship with God (vv. 38-42). Name examples of faith in word and deed.

## Understanding God's Word

In 10:1-24, Jesus sends seventy to announce that "the kingdom of God has come near to you." They represent God's nonviolent reign in saying, "Peace to this house!"

In 10:25-37, the Good Samaritan story answers a question from a religious lawyer. While it is parallel to Matthew 22:34-40 and Mark 12:28-34, the story is unique to Luke. Luke places it on the way to Jerusalem, not in the temple. In Luke, the lawyer cites the commandment to love God and neighbor rather than Jesus. Jesus leads the lawyer to a new understanding of the law and challenges him to "go and do likewise."

Only in Luke (10:38-42) and John do we know about Mary and Martha,

* * * * * * * * * * * * * * * * * * * * * * * * * * * * * * * * *

### For the leader

Ask leaders who direct the church in its evangelistic outreach and those who coordinate its service projects to describe the results of their ministries.

1. Listen as Luke 10:1-12 and 17-20 is read. Assign one person to be the narrator and another Jesus. Suggest, "Imagine that you are one of the seventy. What impressed you about Jesus' instructions? What excited you . . . scared you . . . perplexed you? How do you feel about Jesus' response to their experience?"

2. Pray for one another's involvement in witness and service ministries. Sing a gathering hymn.

sisters who offered hospitality to Jesus. John adds their brother, Lazarus, whose sickness, death, and return to life moved the powers to seek Jesus' death.

## Connecting with God's Word

### *The sending of the seventy (10:1-12)*
The seventy were drawn from unnamed disciples (8:1-3; 23:49). "Seventy" recalls the "table of nations" (Genesis 10), a hint of the universal nature of God's salvation in Jesus.

- How does it feel to be assigned to contact people, knowing that some will be pleased and others will spurn your efforts?

- Seminaries and area conferences encourage congregations to cultivate a "culture of calling" through which youth and young adults consider the call to church leadership. How is this "culture of calling" evident in your church?

- You instruct volunteers on a service assignment. How will Jesus' instructions apply?

### *I saw Satan falling (10:17-20)*
The seventy were overjoyed at their success in healing the sick and casting out demons. The forces hostile to God and capable of doing harm lost their power as disciples announced that "the kingdom of God is near." Jesus cautioned that joy "flows out of our participation in God's heavenly victory of life over Satan" (Richard P. Carlson, *New Proclamation*, Year C, 2004, Easter through Pentecost, Minneapolis: Fortress, 2003, 129.)

- The seventy returned overjoyed at their success. Have you experienced similar joy when someone is healed as the result of your ministry?

### *What must I do? (10:25-28)*
The lawyer likely knew the answer to his question: "What must I do to inherit eternal life?" His question is different in Matthew 22:34-40 and Mark 12:28-31. They report the lawyer asking, "Which commandment in the law is the greatest/first of all?" The answer is the same: "Love God and love neighbor."

### *The Good Samaritan story (10:29-35)*
A man on his way from Jerusalem to Jericho encountered thieves who robbed him, beat him, and left him half-dead. Three travelers saw him. Two religious leaders, a priest and a Levite, were traveling home from the temple. They wouldn't touch a potentially dead person, as that would make them unclean.

But the Samaritan traveler demonstrated compassion by using his oil, wine, bandages, and money.

- Why did the Samaritan stop? What kept the priest and Levite from action? How do you respond to suffering?

- Have you helped a stranded motorist or, when stranded, did a stranger help you?

### The outcome (10:36-37)

Jesus asked the lawyer, "Which of these three do you think was a neighbor?" The lawyer answered rightly, "The one who had mercy on him." The parable answered what loving one's neighbor meant under the law, as a condition for inheriting eternal life—showing mercy, compassion, and care to Jews, Samaritans, and Gentiles alike. Jesus instructed the lawyer to "go and do likewise."

- Jesus said a good neighbor is one who shows mercy to others. None are excused.

- The lawyer wanted to know when his responsibility started and stopped. How does your congregation discern such matters?

### Jesus visits Martha and Mary (Luke 10:38-42)

From John's Gospel we learn that Martha, Mary, and Lazarus lived in Bethany, two miles from Jerusalem. Martha's sister, Mary, sat at the Lord's feet and listened to his teaching. She assumed the position of a disciple, unusual for a woman in that time. Martha was "distracted." She also wanted to receive Jesus' teaching, but was occupied with "her many tasks."

In contrast to these "many tasks," Jesus said that "only one thing" was needed. While hospitality and service are good, the "better part" is heeding the words of Jesus. What Mary chose would "not be taken away from her."

- Substitute your name for Martha's: "_____, _____, you are worried and distracted by many things." List your "many tasks." Do these keep you from the "better part?" How do you balance active and contemplative elements of your faith?

- As you "sit at Jesus' feet," what do worship, reading, education, nature, conversation, and meditation contribute? What other disciplines are helpful?

## Closing

1. Review one ministry of proclamation or service your church has conducted.

2. Close by reading verses 38-42. Pray for guidance to balance daily tasks and spiritual disciplines.

# DEVOTIONALS

* * * * * * * * * * * * * * * * * * * * * * * * * * * * * * * * * * * * * * *

## Devotional 1

*The Lord appointed seventy others and sent them on ahead of him in pairs to every town and place where he himself intended to go.* —*Luke 10:1*

During college one of our outreach projects on Sunday mornings was leafleting houses with a pamphlet called *The Way.* It carried a message of hope and salvation. We walked through neighborhoods before most of the residents were awake. A few people came to the door. I don't recall any negative comments or refusals.

We went in pairs, two by two, just as the disciples did. I was glad for the company of the other person. Their presence calmed my fear and hesitation.

Today, when I lead workshops and retreats, I prefer to work with another person. What I forget, the other usually remembers. Our gifts complement each other. The results are doubled. Afterward, we evaluate the meeting and plan changes for next time.

In our church service, what would happen if two people were assigned to every ministry? Would they be done more conscientiously, with greater accountability? Would the work of the church, and our own effectiveness in God's ministries, be extended? *—Jocele Meyer*

*In our work today, may we find that other person who supports and encourages us in our walk and witness as Christ's disciples.*

## Devotional 2

*Whatever house you enter, first say, "Peace to this house!"* —*Luke 10:5*

When Middle Eastern neighbors meet, one says, "Asalam, Alaykum" (peace be upon you), and the other replies, "Alaykum, Asalam" (upon you, peace). In worship we pass the peace. We say, "Peace be with you," and the other responds, "And also with you."

How about using this greeting in daily life? At your next dinner party or visit to a friend you could begin the encounter with the words of Jesus: "Peace to this house! . . . The kingdom of God has come near to you!"

This is a calming word for our tumultuous times. It may be used during patriotic holidays like July 1 (Canada) or July 4 (USA), when the military is often glorified. As it was for the disciples, so it is for us: Our work must begin and end with the peace and love of Jesus so that we can share the kingdom of God with all whom we meet. *—Lauren Mayfield*

*God, thank you for inviting us to work alongside you while spreading your peace around the world. Empower us to represent the kingdom of God well. Asalam, Alaykum!*

* * * * * * * * * * * * * * *

## Devotional 3

*Rejoice that your names are written in heaven. —Luke 10:20*

A famous golfer, Tiger Woods, once lamented that everyone made too much of both his winning and losing. The wins were inflated in importance, and the losses were overly criticized. Of course Woods wanted to win, but when he didn't, life went on.

Returning from their ministry trip, the disciples misplaced the importance of their actions. They were pleased about the spiritual power they had been given. Jesus affirmed their success but cautioned: "Do not rejoice at this. . . . but rejoice that your names are written in heaven."

As with Tiger Woods, we can put too much stock in our own spiritual successes and failures. We may be tempted to take too much credit when our service to God goes well and too much blame when it doesn't.

Jesus' words remind us to rejoice in the right things. Success is good, but not guaranteed. So I simply thank God for the chance to serve, and even more, for God's eternal love. *–Philip Wiebe*

*Lord, forgive me for thinking too much of my own status and success as I serve others. May I simply serve with joy, giving you all of the glory and honor.*

* * * * * * * * * * * * * *

## Devotional 4

*Blessed are the eyes that see what you see! Many prophets and kings desired to see what you see. —Luke 10:23b-24*

In our home we knew that it was our parents who put presents under the tree, not Santa Claus. Sometimes they placed them there a few days before Christmas. I would sit on the floor by the hour, shaking packages that had my name written on them.

During Advent, we focus on waiting. For centuries, the Jewish community waited for the Promised One. They thought their coming king would be a strong political ruler who would conquer all of Israel's enemies.

Instead, Jesus first reveals himself to the simple folk of the Galilean countryside. In his prayer (v. 21), Jesus indicates that God is revealed to those who are prepared to follow him. It is a gift hidden from those who do not intend to follow him.

His followers see what the prophets and kings desired to see but did not recognize. May that be our experience during Advent. *–Joanne Lehman*

*As I wrap packages and keep secrets during this Advent season, give me eyes to see Jesus and ears to hear the good news of the kingdom of God.*

* * * * * * * * * * * * * * *

## Devotional 5

*Love . . . your neighbor as yourself. —Luke 10:27*

I've heard and read the parable of the Good Samaritan so many times I'm almost immune to its message. I thought I had nothing more to say about or learn from this story—until a new family moved in next door.

They were of a different culture. There was constant traffic to and from the house. We weren't sure how many people lived in the house. There were acts of vandalism on our street that had never happened before. Other neighbors started talking about the disruption of our quiet suburban life. What should we do? Should we call the police? Ignore them? Confront them?

We decided to throw a block party

instead. Almost everyone around the block came. We learned each others' names and appreciated our various backgrounds. We had a great time eating and visiting well into the evening.

There are lots of things we can do to be good neighbors to all people around the world. Sometimes the best place to start is right next door! *—Gareth Brandt*

*Lord, help me to be a good neighbor to those across the street and around the world.*

* * * * * * * * * * * * * *

## Devotional 6

*"Which of these three . . . was a neighbor?". . . He said, "The one who showed him mercy." Jesus said to him, "Go and do likewise." —Luke 10:36-37*

One Hanukkah young Isaac stenciled a menorah on his bedroom window. Suddenly, flying bricks shattered the window. The police advised the Jewish family to remove the symbol to avoid further violence. But Isaac's mother felt that giving in to hatred wasn't right.

The local media featured this story. It touched the heart of a Christian mother who contacted her pastor. Christians all over town responded by putting menorahs in their windows. The newspaper printed a menorah that residents cut out and displayed. Jewish and Christian friendship grew as they worked together to affirm that love is stronger than hatred.

Jesus knew the lawyer was an expert in Jewish law. Instead of debating, Jesus appealed to his heart by telling the parable of the Samaritan, a traditional enemy who modeled neighbor-love.

As then, many communities experience hate crimes among ethnic groups. Religious and ethnic tensions fuel most wars. And yet,

simple acts of compassion and solidarity can lead to healing. *—Annie Lind*

*Compassionate Christ, touch our hearts and set them on fire with your love, especially toward those who are different from us.*

* * * * * * * * * * * * * *

## Devotional 7

*Mary has chosen the better part, which will not be taken away from her. —Luke 10:42*

I have a friend who loves me. She never misses giving me birthday and Christmas gifts. She invites me to her parties and comes to mine. She has a lot of food prepared when I go to her place. We spend a lot of time together, but I don't say much. We stay busy doing things.

I have another friend who loves me. She finds ways for us to spend more time together. She rarely cooks, but she'll pick up a cup of my favorite coffee on her way over, so we can have more time together. She listens to me with such a fascinated presence that I want to tell her everything . . . and I do! I know that what I say will be cherished and honored as holy. She trusts me with her pain and joy as well.

When I want someone to really listen to me, I am drawn to this second friend. She helps me understand why Jesus would say that Mary chose the one thing that was needed. He needed a listening ear. He still does! *—Sandra Drescher-Lehman*

*What kind of friend do you most enjoy? To whom can you give that kind of friendship today?*

# Practicing humility and hospitality

## LUKE 14

### Opening

This session features a wedding banquet and the great dinner. How do you prepare occasions for friends, relatives, and special guests? Such events often involve a theme, food, entertainment, venue, and a program. What event have you planned and hosted recently? What surprised you? What did you learn?

### Understanding the Word

Luke 14:1-24 includes four teaching vignettes that Jesus told at a Sabbath meal with a prominent Pharisee. At this dinner Jesus had another event in mind—the messianic banquet at the end of the age.

He tells two parables. The first (vv. 7-14) is about choosing places of honor at a wedding banquet. The second (vv. 15-24) is about the great banquet feast in heaven. Both teach the reversal of human expectations. In both, Jesus teaches about humility and hospitality.

Jesus invites guests to live now in accordance with God's coming reign; for "in the kingdom God is host, and who can repay God?" (Fred B. Craddock, *Harper's Bible Commentary*, HarperSanFrancisco, 1988, 1,033).

### For the leader

Interview an event planner. Learn what is involved in hosting an event that contributes to the life of the church.

1. Pray for one another's witness to the gospel in humble and hospitable ways. Sing a gathering hymn.

2. Invite the class to stand as you read the parable of the wedding banquet, Luke 14:7-14. Be seated. Then read the parable of the great dinner, verses 15-24.

Verses 25-35 conclude chapter 14 with Jesus' call for all to become his disciples. Discipleship involves sharing Christ's suffering and living as his servant. As Jesus went to the cross, those who follow him must be willing to go likewise. Jesus asks hearers to count the cost before saying "yes."

## Connecting with God's Word

### *Parables of humility and hospitality (14:1-14)*

In 13:29 Jesus said, "People will come from east and west and from north and south, and will eat in the kingdom of God." Jesus taught that God's feast was both in the future and here, now. In his comments, Jesus:

1. Acted in direct conflict with the moral code of his host (vv. 1-6). He healed a man with dropsy on the Sabbath. Compassion was more important than purity.

2. Introduced the etiquette of God's reign. He also criticized party manners (vv. 7-11). Jesus noticed that some weren't waiting to be seated and chose places on their own.

3. Criticized the guest list (vv. 12-14). He urged the host to invite those who could not repay the favor. In effect Jesus said, "While you won't be repaid in this life, you will be the fortunate ones, for you will be showing that you 'get it.' You know God's reign and you're living into it."

4. Burst one guest's bubble (vv. 15ff.). The guest exclaimed, "Blessed is one who will eat bread in the kingdom of God!" (v. 15). He had the messianic banquet in mind, but thought it was to come. He was waiting for the day, confident that he would be there.

- What are the places of honor in your church and your community? Who occupies them?

- How do people sit in your worship services and fellowship meals? Do role or rank affect these arrangements?

- How does your congregation show hospitality to outsiders?

- How does your congregation demonstrate humility and hospitality to the homeless?

- Was Jesus recommending a more effective strategy in the parable of the wedding banquet? "Start low. That way you'll draw honor to yourself when your host tells you to take a better spot." Note that verse 11 is describing kingdom behavior.

***Parable of the great dinner (14:15-24)***

Three groups are represented:

The first group is the well-to-do, busy, and polite. They said yes to the invitation. They intend to participate in God's future party. But right now they have many good and necessary things to handle: houses, gardens, travel, work, computers, and relationships. Not today but maybe tomorrow … the next day … or next year …

The second group is those who experience unbelievable joy, know a party is happening but never expected to be invited: (1) the man with dropsy; (2) the poor, blind, crippled, and lame in Jesus' society and ours; and (3) lay people who sit in church year after year and feel like wallflowers.

The third group is the utterly surprised, who didn't know there was a party. They can't believe they are compelled to come.

- Isaiah 25:6-10 describes the messianic banquet. This rich feast is open for everyone!

- While God's reign, symbolized in a great banquet, is in the future, it is for people today.

- The banquet invitation is sent. The invitation must be answered immediately. What are the "decisive moments" for you? For your congregation?

- How does the Lord's Supper point to the messianic banquet? Could your congregation incorporate the messianic banquet into its observance?

- Why don't we invite outsiders to join the party? Why is the host in a hurry (v. 23)? What is your level of urgency for mission?

- The episode ends when Jesus finishes the second parable (v. 24). Was Jesus speaking about you? What do these parables add to your understanding of the gospel?

- Who are your "outsiders," not freely participating in the life of the community (recent immigrants, divorced persons, former prisoners, single-parent families, lonely seniors, youth who hang out in the mall)? How could your church reach them?

## Closing

1. Name one way you intend to express hospitality in your home and/or community this week.

2. Pray for a spirit of humility as you extend hospitality to "outsiders."

3. As a sending admonition, read verses 21-24 (begin with "Go out at once…"). Sing a sending hymn.

*Luke 14*

# DEVOTIONALS

* * * * * * * * * * * * * * * * * *

## Devotional 1

*When Jesus was going to the house of a leader of the Pharisees to eat a meal on the Sabbath, they were watching him closely. —Luke 14:1*

I'm not famous. I can meet a friend without fear of my image being splashed across the tabloids. These papers love to catch celebrities at their worst—not unlike the Pharisees.

The Pharisees revered God's law and the traditions that protected it. Jesus was a threat. They assumed they could orchestrate his downfall. Perhaps they arranged for the man with dropsy to be in Jesus' way, hoping Jesus would become the latest tabloid scandal.

But Jesus was not worried about being caught. He focused on the sick man with compassion, aware of the Pharisees' intent. Jesus used the man's healing to teach the Pharisees.

Jesus hoped those eager for the law would see how to practice it. The Pharisees were silenced by his actions and his questions.

Do people see God's truth in me? While I am not a celebrity, people such as neighbors, children, and co-workers watch how I live. What do they see? *—Susan Fish*

*Jesus, help me to put aside fears of what others will think of me and focus on being like you in your love of truth and people.*

* * * * * * * * * * * * * *

## Devotional 2

*All who exalt themselves will be humbled, and those who humble themselves will be exalted. —Luke 14:11*

I raised my hand when the professor asked,

"Who read today's assignment?" Not having done so but wanting to appear knowledgeable, I raised my hand. Of course, the professor asked me to explain the reading—which I could not. I was shamed by my own dishonesty.

We are often expected to show confidence when we do not feel confident. We don't want to appear weak. We don't like to answer, "I don't know." But when we act like we know everything, we miss life's opportunities.

Jesus says that it is better to be exalted by our humility than to be humbled by our self-exaltation. He applies this to our relationship with God. When we come to God and claim that we are okay, we close ourselves to God's blessings. When we come to God with a humble heart, we can receive God's healing word.

Those who say, "I don't know," to God can become closer to God. *—Adam S. Yoder*

*God, grant me the strength to be weak. Grant me the courage to be humble. Grant me the love I need to join the needy. Grant me the trust I need to be vulnerable.*

* * * * * * * * * * * * * *

## Devotional 3

*When you give a banquet, invite the poor, the crippled, the lame, and the blind. —Luke 14:13*

Missionaries in Nepal described what God is doing in the church there. I remembered one thing. In this caste-ridden society, the communion meal is distinctive and unique. Former Brahmins (the Hindu highest caste) eat with those who once were considered untouchable.

Jesus' list of whom to invite to a party (v. 13) is not just a random collection of guests. It is a deliberate reference to those who are disqualified from the priestly office (Leviticus 21:21). These formed the underclass of first-century Jewish society.

Jesus' ministry is explicitly to people like this (Luke 4:18-19; 7:22; 14:13, 21). Jesus calls us to a radical subversion of structures and systems that exclude and marginalize people.

Who are on the margins of our society—the refugee, the homeless, the AIDS patient? Whose sins have put them beyond the pale—the rapist, the terrorist, the child abuser?

Should we associate with such people? Is Jesus really asking this of us? —*Helen Paynte*

*Jesus, you are the expert at reaching the excluded. Teach me how to tear down the boundaries around my heart and my life.*

* * * * * * * * * * * * * * *

## Devotional 4

*I tell you, none of those invited will taste my dinner. —Luke 14:24*

With our menu of emails, texting, and smart phones, the fast food of technology can leave us famished. A 21st century scenario of this parable reminds me that God calls me to the lavish table of retreat and I respond: "I must meet this deadline; I'm sorry. I must meet my friend at the gym; please accept my apologies; I cannot come."

I get entangled in the Web, zone out in front of television, or chat on email. This constant diet of outside stimulus makes our spiritual disciplines tasteless, just as a diet of sugar makes eating fruits and vegetables difficult.

Consider how our temporal busyness can keep us from tasting God's banquet (v. 24). We may be absent from the party because we've starved ourselves by not eating God's

Word. The great dinner is ready for those who take the time to come (v. 14). We can decline the fast food of technology and taste the fine wines and nutritious breads from heaven. —*Laurie Oswald Robinson*

*Host of the great dinner, wean us from the lure of the emptiness of spiritual "fast food." Teach us to feast on your ways, your Self.*

* * * * * * * * * * * * * * *

## Devotional 5

*[Jesus said,] "Whoever does not carry the cross and follow me cannot be my disciple." —Luke 14:27*

Dr. Paul Brand spent a lifetime in the treatment of leprosy in southwestern India. Many patients were blind or missing hands or feet. Most were beggars who could not pay for their treatment.

Dr. Brand discovered that leprosy destroys nerve endings. He and his spouse, Margaret, spent years correcting deformities of the hands and feet through tendon transfers. They remade human noses, replaced lost eyebrows, and prevented blindness by restoring the ability to blink.

Dr. Brand took delight in "losing" his life in serving the powerless. In *Soul Survivor*, he said, "Because of where I practiced medicine, I never made much money. . . . Those of us who involve ourselves in places where there is much suffering look back to find that it was there that we discovered the reality of joy."

May Dr. Brand's story inspire us to "give up all [our] possessions" (v. 33) to follow Jesus. In giving, we understand the gospel paradox that it is in giving that we receive. —*Bob Hoffman*

*"Riches I heed not nor vain empty praise. Thou my inheritance, now and always. Thou and thou only, first in my heart, high King*

of heaven, my treasure thou art." —Ancient
Irish hymn "Be thou my vision," number 545
in Hymnal: A Worship Book (Scottdale, PA:
Mennonite Publishing House, 1992).

## Devotional 6

*Which of you, intending to build a tower,
does not first sit down and estimate the cost?
— Luke 14:28*

My contractor friend determines the cost
of building a new home. His college course
taught him how to consider every detail and
the way to show homeowners how changes
affect the final cost.

When building a house, one must follow
the budget. Jesus laid out a similar message:
Estimate the cost of being a disciple. If you
begin the faith journey, follow it.

When I became a Christian at age 12
I did not calculate my decision. Three years
later, in a baptismal class, I considered the
faith more critically. I needed to know the
implications of being baptized and becoming
a congregational member.

During high school, I was baptized. While
I didn't have solid answers to my questions,
my commitment to Christ outweighed the
implications I was considering.

I said, "Yes I will follow Jesus, whatever
the cost, whatever the questions, and trust
that I will have the faith and means to finish
what I started." *–Jill Landis*

*Caller of disciples, I want to give all I have
to follow you, but sometimes I am afraid of
what it will mean. Help me build my faith on
you, no matter the cost.*

## Devotional 7

*This fellow began to build and was not able
to finish. —Luke 14:30*

In baseball, there is no lonelier spot than
the outfield when the crack of a bat sends
a towering fly ball on its way. The eyes of
all spectators–parents, significant other, or
pro-scouts–follow the path of the ball.

The potential for disgrace is limitless.
There's no way to redeem a failed catch.
Little wonder that the sports lingo, "finishing
well," lingers with outfielders.

Where Christians are a suspect minority,
the potential for humiliating collapse under
pressure is always present. They are
vulnerable to public scorn everywhere in
the streets, markets, and courts. Negotiat-
ing each day can be a lonely, depleting affair.

Jesus' brusque challenge is that Christians must prepare for long-haul, high-risk
demands. They do so by getting rid of their
resources. Jesus says, "None of you can
become my disciple if you do not give up all
your possessions" (v. 33). The stamina for
success will come from beyond us–as a gift.
*–Jonathan Larson*

*"But I know whom I have believed, and am
persuaded that [God] is able to keep that
which I've committed unto him against that
day." —"I know not why God's wondrous,"
number 338 in Hymnal: A Worship Book
(Scottdale, PA: Mennonite Publishing
House, 1992).*

# 8

# Service—the way of greatness

* * * * * * * * * * * * * * * * * * * * * * * * * * * * * *

## Opening

Jesus transformed the Passover meal into the Lord's Supper (vv. 7-23). Christians observe it to celebrate Jesus' life, suffering, death, and resurrection. How central is this event in your church?

## Understanding God's Word

Judas agrees to deliver Jesus to the leaders (vv. 1-6); verses 7-23 describe the Passover and Lord's Supper; Jesus describes the essence of greatness as servanthood (vv. 24-30); Jesus predicts Peter's denial (vv. 31-34); and the prophecy that "Jesus was counted among the lawless" (vv. 35-38) is fulfilled. On the Mount of Olives (vv. 39-46) Jesus is betrayed and arrested (vv. 47-53); Peter denies Jesus (54-62); the authorities reject Jesus (vv. 63-71); and Jesus is crucified.

Jesus fulfills the Passover meal in the Lord's Supper. The disciples look back to Jesus' suffering and ahead to the great dinner at the end of the age. This meal, "in remembrance of me" (1 Corinthians 11:25), is a communal activity. It makes real the presence of Christ and the kingdom.

### Terms related to the Lord's Supper

- Eucharist: From eucharistein, "to give thanks." Term used for the Lord's Supper.
- Feast of the Unleavened Bread: Jewish holy week after Passover
- Maundy Thursday: From mande, "mandate" and "command." The Night of the Commandment describes Jesus' plans for the Lord's Supper.
- Passion Narrative: From paschein, "to suffer." All Gospels include it.
- Passover: Translated from the Hebrew pesach (Greek pascha). Recalls the angel of death "passing over," sparing the Israelites before the Exodus.

## For the leader

Ask your pastor to explain Lord's Supper and footwashing observances.

1. Pray for wisdom and healing of the concerns of this week. Sing a gathering hymn.

2. Read Luke 22:7-13. How does your church prepare for the Lord's Supper? Read verses 14-20. The Lord's Supper is a ritual established by Jesus to help us remember Christ's activity for us.

## Connecting with God's Word

### *When the hour came (Luke 22:14-16)*

The feast remembering the Jewish exodus from Egypt was transformed into a celebration of Jesus' exodus. Jesus longed to observe Passover (pascha) with them before he suffered (paschein). When observed, this meal looks backward to Jesus' suffering and forward to the great dinner of God's kingdom.

In this meal, Jesus substituted his body for the sacrificial lamb and his blood for the blood sprinkled on the people at Sinai (Exodus 24:8): "the cup that is poured out for you is the new covenant in my blood" (v. 20). In breaking the bread and passing the cup, Jesus invited followers to a communal meal.

- Eating is important. How do families and churches celebrate their meals?

- Have you witnessed communion (eucharist) in other congregations? What meanings were emphasized? What does your congregation emphasize?

- Some congregations share a seder meal prior to communion. How does the seder contribute to your understanding of communion?

- In the bread and the cup, Jesus invites all to experience his presence. How is Jesus present in your observance?

### *The hand of the one who is going to betray me is with mine on the table (22:21-23)*

Jesus denounced the betrayer even though his action was "determined." The disciples asked, "Who would do this?" (v. 23).

- Believers can turn against Christ through words and deeds. How do you overcome this temptation?

### *A dispute arose among them (22:24-27)*

When Jesus introduced the kingdom, the disciples disputed about who would be greatest. Jesus reminded them that while pagans "lord it over" their subjects, he forbade such display of power. Jesus insisted that authority is exercised through service. Jesus washed their feet (John 13:1-17) to illustrate his teaching.

### I confer on you a kingdom (22:28-30)
Jesus conferred on them a kingdom of service. Eating and drinking in the great dinner would be "at my table in my kingdom" and they would judge from the "twelve thrones" (Matthew 19:28) of the new Israel.

### But I have prayed for you, Simon (22:31-32)
"Simon, Simon," Jesus said, "Satan has demanded to sift you as wheat." Jesus' prayer was that, though Peter might fail, "your faith may not fail." Peter's experience would make him a better servant/leader among the believers.

### Today, you will deny three times that you know me (22:33-34)
Peter declared he would go with Jesus to prison and death. Jesus predicted that Peter would deny him.

### This man was with him (22:54-60)
Peter follows Jesus "at a distance." First, a servant girl recognizes him: "This man was with him." Peter insists, "Woman, I do not know him!" (v. 57). Second, a servant accuses: "You also are one of them." "Man, I am not!" (v. 60) replies Peter. Third, Peter is recognized as a Galilean (Matthew 26:73) because of his accent. Peter denies, "I do not know what you are talking about!" Then the rooster crows.

### The Lord looked at Peter who "went outside and wept bitterly" (22: 61-62)
Peter disappears from the trial, crucifixion, and burial events. We meet him next running toward an empty tomb. Peter is someone whom Christ loves and calls, despite weaknesses.

- Do you sometimes see Peter's actions in your own?

## Closing

1. Name one way that the Lord's Supper and footwashing have inspired your life of service.
2. Read John 13:1-17. Thank God for the many ways others serve you. Pray for readiness to serve others by the example of Christ.

# DEVOTIONALS

* * * * * * * * * * * * * * * * * *

## Devotional 1

*They were afraid of the people. —Luke 22:2b*

The fear of the people forced evildoers to find secret ways to commit their crimes. Judas and the religious leaders knew that a crowd could see through their murderous plot.

Most crimes take place in secret. A crowd deters a street criminal. Neighborhood watches and safe houses keep perpetrators from criminal actions. Institutions need monitors to keep them honest and just. Citizens review laws and challenge those that are unfair.

International observers reduce human rights abuses. Christian Peacemaker Teams (CPT) oppose leaders who harass native peoples. CPT members conduct night watches to prevent soldiers and police from violating citizens. CPT members listen to the stories of the oppressed. Churches are matched with families in occupied territories so they can publicize their plights. Knowing that someone sees what is happening offers hope to those suffering injustice.

Letters to editors and contact with officials let them know that we see their actions. Ordinary people have much power to expose and prevent violence when they work together. *–Susan Balzer*

*Omnipresent God, give me the courage to watch out for vulnerable people in my community and to expose evil, even when it involves people in high positions.*

## Devotional 2

*Jesus sent Peter and John, saying, "Go and prepare the Passover meal for us that we may eat it." — Luke 22:8*

It was important to Jesus' disciples that they eat the Passover meal together. Commemoration of the Israelites' liberation from slavery was central to their faith and identity.

The disciples were in the holy city, Jerusalem. Jesus took care of the arrangements and assigned them to prepare the meal. Together they would share special foods, sing the blessed psalms, remember Passovers past, and reflect on God's redeeming work.

My wife Jennie and I attended seminary in the Midwest, more than two thousand miles away from my home on the West Coast. Like us, other students didn't have the time or the money to return to their families for Thanksgiving, Christmas, or Easter.

We took the initiative to ensure that none of us spent these holidays alone. We prepared a turkey for Thanksgiving, chili for Christmas, and a ham for Easter. We invited others to share the day with us. Together we commemorated God's love on each special day. *–Frank Ramirez*

*Whether you are living close to your roots or far away, ponder the ways in which you can share holidays with God's people.*

* * * * * * * * * * * * * * *

## Devotional 3

*They went and found everything as he had told them; and they prepared the Passover meal. —Luke 22:13*

We see God's providence and sense of humor displayed. A man carrying a jar of water! What could be more specific and incongruous? Men didn't carry water; women did.

Peter and John did not question Jesus' instructions, for only a few days earlier the disciples had found the colt that Jesus needed exactly where he said it would be.

Jesus, who promised to prepare a place for his followers in heaven, depended on others to provide the upper room for his final Passover feast. The one who gives believers a heavenly home had no home on earth.

Jesus asked for what he needed, and God provided a homeowner to share exactly what was needed.

Have you experienced God's providence? Jesus taught us to ask God to supply our needs—confidently and specifically. God may answer our prayers in ways that surprise us, just as the sight of a man carrying water must have amazed Peter and John. —Susan Balzer

*Father, hallowed be your name. . . . Give us each day our daily bread. . . . Forgive us our sins, for we ourselves forgive everyone indebted to us. . . . And do not bring us to the time of trial. (Luke 11:2-4)*

\* \* \* \* \* \* \* \* \* \* \* \* \* \* \*

# Devotional 4

*When the hour came, [Jesus] took his place at the table, and the apostles with him. —Luke 22:14*

Sometimes guys get together in the kitchen and have a good time. In our church in Los Angeles we had a group of men who enjoyed cooking. Our cooking always led to getting together with the women as well.

Kenny Miller would lay out 20 pans on the burners and make eggs for everyone at the Easter breakfast. Bill Forney taught me that when you prepare a church meal, the best way to celebrate is to get high-quality food and treat your guests like royalty. After all, this is the body of Christ.

Jesus and the apostles met together for the Passover meal, celebrating the journey from slavery to freedom, and instituting a new meal commemorating our liberation from the slavery of sin.

Table fellowship is at the heart of our Christian faith, whether men and women, Jew and Gentile, rich and poor, or slave and free. We are one people called together at God's table. By eating together we are fully God's people. —*Frank Ramirez*

*God of all, bless us beyond our comfort level so that if we say we wish to include everyone, you will send us everyone to share our table.*

\* \* \* \* \* \* \* \* \* \* \* \* \* \* \*

# Devotional 5

*This is my body, which is given for you. —Luke 22:19*

I am strengthened in the communion service knowing that Jesus gave his life for us. The Passover meal was a reenactment of the Israelites being freed from Egypt's power. As the disciples ate they must have hoped to be freed from Rome's power.

Imagine their shock when Jesus broke the unleavened bread and said, "This is my body, which is given for you." They knew Jesus' life was under threat but they kept thinking, he'll pull us through. Now Jesus was saying that he would be killed.

Only after his crucifixion and resurrection did they ponder the meaning of these words. Jesus said to do this "in remembrance" (v. 19) of him. Like the Passover meal, it is a reenactment, a way to instill the awareness that Jesus is present with us.

The body Jesus gave was given "for us." Jesus' sacrificial love is hard to imagine, but it is what God calls us to reenact every day. Communion strengthens us to do this.
—Gordon Houser

*Lord Jesus, we thank you for giving your life for us, and we commit ourselves to live out that kind of love.*

\* \* \* \* \* \* \* \* \* \* \* \* \* \* \*

## Devotional 6

*A dispute also arose among them as to which one of them was to be regarded as the greatest. —Luke 22:24*

As a youth my study of world history was Europe and USA-centered. It focused on great battles and great people. As an adult I've learned that history is about the way in which ordinary people, in many cultures, lived every day.

For thousands of years the indigenous peoples of the Four Corners region of Utah, Colorado, Arizona, and New Mexico were hunters and gatherers. They built pit houses, settled in, then moved on with their few possessions to another place.

Recently I studied the Ancestral Pueblo people. From around AD 800 to 1300, they built complex structures aligned with the movements of the sun and moon. Pueblo Bonito in Chaco Canyon, the largest struc- ture in North America until the late 19th century, has more than six hundred rooms and is over five stories tall.

The apostles argued about who is the greatest in terms of the world's under- standing of power and importance. Jesus, however, taught that greatness involves turning the world's perspective upside down. It's the same for us too.
—Frank Ramirez

*Day by day, dear Lord, of thee three things I pray: to see thee more clearly, love thee more dearly, follow thee more nearly, day by day.*
*—St. Richard of Chichester*

\* \* \* \* \* \* \* \* \* \* \* \* \* \* \*

## Devotional 7

*The Lord turned and looked at Peter. Then Peter remembered the word of the Lord, how he had said to him. —Luke 22:61*

In *Paddle to the Amazon*, a father and two sons attempt to paddle their canoe from the Red River near Winnipeg, Canada, to the mouth of the Amazon River. The big test comes when one son decides to return home.

When things became too difficult for Peter, he forgot the promise of Christ's resurrection and victory. He didn't want to face the questioning, the taunting, and the arrest.

I can't accuse Peter of cowardice, for I too have found it easier to make promises and commitments in the company of friends than to openly express my faith to unbelievers. Jesus was exposed not only to verbal questioning like Peter, but also to physical punishment and scorn. But Jesus did not desert his Father.

In *Paddle to the Amazon*, the second son remained with his father throughout the journey. They celebrated the end of the trip together. Christ has promised a successful ending to our journey with him. I need this daily reminder to not give up.
—Edith Ratzlaff

*God, keep me, not only from pride, but also from the sin of protecting myself with lies. Give me an honest, humble heart and help me to be faithful to the end.*

CPSIA information can be obtained at www.ICGtesting.com
Printed in the USA
BVOW031317200112

280811BV00005B/8/P